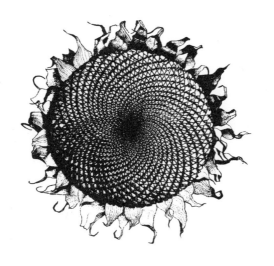

THE SUNFLOWER

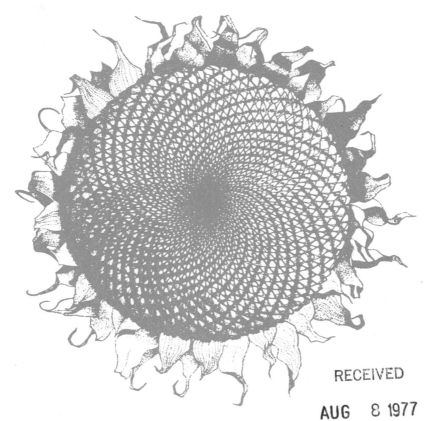

THE SUNFLOWER

CHARLES B. HEISER, JR.

UNIVERSITY OF OKLAHOMA PRESS · NORMAN

By Charles B. Heiser, Jr.

Nightshades: The Paradoxical Plants (San Francisco, 1969)

Seed to Civilization: The Story of Man's Food (San Francisco, 1973)

The Sunflower (Norman, 1976)

QK
495
.C74
H43

Library of Congress Cataloging in Publication Data

Heiser, Charles Bixler, 1920–
    The sunflower.

    Includes bibliographical references and index. 1.   Sunflowers.
I.   Title.
QK495.C74H43   583'.55   74–15906
ISBN 0–8061–1229–8

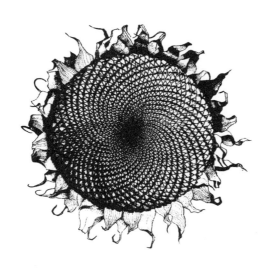

To My Students

I hope that they have learned much from me.
I know that I have learned much from them.

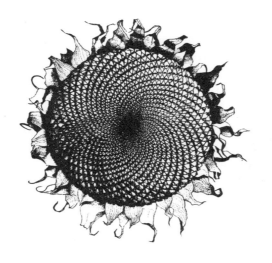

Foreword: Mostly Personal

THE following account of the sunflower is not a complete one, nor is it intended to be. I hope that it is, however, an accurate and informative one. Other chapters based on our present knowledge could be written, and there will be new chapters for the future, for much remains to be discovered about sunflowers.

My study of sunflowers began in 1942, when I was a junior at Washington University, in St. Louis, Missouri. Having already decided to become a botanist, I was enrolled in an advanced course taught by Professor Edgar Anderson, who was recognized as an eminent geneticist and student of evolution. Professor Anderson was also an outstanding teacher, although a somewhat unorthodox one. The course in which I studied with him that fall was devoted solely to the composite family. We studied asters, goldenrods, chicory, and many other composites, but it was sunflowers that occupied most of our attention. It was on a field trip to a vacant lot in South St. Louis to look at sunflowers that Professor Anderson said to me, "Charley, if someone looked into sunflowers very carefully, he would discover something significant," or words to that effect. That remark stuck with me, and a few years later I realized that it was more than a casual remark on his part. He was deeply interested in sunflowers, he wanted someone to make an intensive study of them, and he knew how to arouse my interest. I also later realized that he could have made the same remark about almost any group of plants, and it would be true.

Although I did not use sunflowers as the subject for my master's dissertation at Washington University, my interest in them continued, and in this I had the constant encouragement of Professor Anderson. These were the years of World War II. Because of gasoline rationing travel was limited, and so my study of sunflowers was largely confined to examining them on vacant lots and railroad yards around St. Louis and East St. Louis. Professor Anderson did, however, secure a small grant of money from the Missouri Botanical Garden that enabled me to make a trip by bus to Arizona. The specific object of the trip was to learn as much as possible about the sunflowers cultivated by the Hopi Indians. I did not get to see the Hopi sunflower on that trip, but the common sunflower and *Helianthus petiolaris* both grew near the Museum of Northern Arizona, which had provided me with lodging. I noted some unusual variants among these plants, but I thought nothing more about them at the time, perhaps because I was having such a wonderful time looking at so many plants new to me in the Arizona flora. I did, however, make herbarium specimens of the sunflowers for later study.

On my return home I resolved to learn more about *H. petiolaris*, a population of which grew near a streetcar stop I frequented on my way to the university. One day the following year I was riding the streetcar, and about two blocks from the university I observed a few depauperate plants that

Edgar Anderson examines a sunflower with Dale Smith, in the author's garden in 1954.

somehow looked different from either the common sunflower or *H. petiolaris*. I pushed the buzzer, got off at the next stop, and walked back to look at the sunflowers. The more I examined them the more convinced I became that they had to be hybrids between the two species. After sleeping on my discovery, I went to tell Professor Anderson about it, and he was as excited as I was. I was delighted in more than one way, for it was the first time I was able to tell Professor Anderson anything about sunflowers that he did not already know. Later, pulling out my herbarium specimens from Arizona, I found that my "unusual variants" from there were also hybrids. Of course, one might use the finding of the hybrids in St. Louis to point out that it is not always necessary to go to an exotic place to find something interesting.

When I left Washington University in 1945 to go to the University of California to earn my Ph.D. degree, I made the trip by train. I saw thousands of sunflowers on the way, and it was frustrating not to be able to examine them. As we came into California, I became aware that the sunflowers had smaller heads than those that I had been seeing previously. As the train stopped in the station at Hanford, I realized that the last sunflowers I had seen were only a quarter of a mile away, and I ran back to collect a few plants. I cannot imagine what my fellow passengers thought of the strange young man who came back carrying a bouquet of sunflowers, but I got to look at the sunflowers closely, and they were later to figure in my Ph.D. thesis. After receiving my degree from California—based primarily on a study of hybridization of the common sunflower with the western species, *H. bolanderi*, I went in 1947 to Indiana University, which has been my home base for research since that time.

Some of the most enjoyable parts of my work have been the field trips. I have always felt that to understand a plant one must see it growing naturally as well as in the garden or greenhouse. My trips have taken me to most parts of the United States and into Mexico and the Andes as well. An account of my travels does not make particularly exciting reading and cannot compare with those left to us by some of the earlier botanists of their collecting expeditions. I usually traveled by automobile and stayed at motels rather than camping out, because I could work better with the plants in a motel room. In addition, I could cover more ground than if I camped out and had to prepare meals.

My family did not always share my enthusiasm for sunflowers, for often on trips with them I would see a sunflower that I had to examine. They would have to sit in the car in the hot sun while I investigated, but they were generally pretty good sports about it. I didn't realize what sunflowers meant to my daughter until one fall day when I was getting ready to drive her to school. Getting into the car, I looked over at a row of *H. maximiliani* that I had planted in the back yard.

"Isn't that a beautiful plant?" I asked her.

"Oh, not particularly," she answered.

"Why not?"

"I don't think so," she replied, "for I have been seeing sunflowers as long as I have been able to see."

The search for rare or little-known species I have found to be particularly interesting, although I must admit that the study of the rare species is no more important, or perhaps even less so, than that of the more common species. Before setting out, I would, of course, have some knowledge of where the rare species grew from the study of herbarium records, and usually my search was successful. But I have never found *H. praetermissus*, which has been collected only once, at Rio Laguna, New Mexico, in 1851. Perhaps it is extinct.

In 1954 my wife and I set out for the Southwest, and I hoped particularly to obtain seeds of *H. anomalus* and of the Hopi sunflower. I knew that the former occurred in both Monument Valley and the Hopi Indian Reservation. Although we drove the length of Monument Valley and saw magnificent scenery, there was not a sunflower to be seen. Going from there to the Hopi country, we at length found the plant for which I was searching. But there was only a single plant, and it was not in seed. Indeed, it is unlikely that it would produce any seed, for there was not another sunflower in the vicinity that could have served as the pollen parent. I did get buds for a chromosome count, however.

Time was getting short, and I decided to abandon the search for *H. anomalus* and concentrate on the Hopi sunflower. As we drove through the Hopis' country, all my inquiries about where I could find their cultivated sunflower received the same answer. They no longer grew it. Finally in the village of Old Oraibi I asked the schoolteacher if he could help me. He said he did not know anything about the sunflower but that he would get a boy who could take me through-

The author (*seated, with hat*) explaining sunflowers to a class in 1954.

out the village. The boy was not too hopeful of results, for he said that very few people still grew the sunflower. At least that was more encouraging than the previous answers. I still did not have too much hope of getting seed, for it was the middle of the summer, the new crop would not be ripe, and the Indians might have planted all the old seeds, but at least I might make arrangements to have seeds sent to me at some later date. The boy's inquiries finally led us to the house of an old woman. Yes, she might have some seeds, I learned from the boy, for the old woman spoke no English (or would not speak it to me). She invited us into the house and took a jar from a shelf. She then walked to the center of the room, got down on her knees, and poured the contents of the jar on the floor. Out rolled a mixture of seeds—several varieties of squashes, beans, and, I was happy to see, sunflowers. I pointed to a sunflower achene, and the woman smiled. I had a feeling that she did not think I would be able to distinguish it from the other seeds.

So the trip was far from a failure. I also collected seeds of several other species, and I am happy to add that eventually I did get seeds of *H. anomalus*. A former student of mine, Warren Stoutamire, was in the area later and was able to collect seeds. Over the years many other individuals have supplied me with seeds of various species, which have been of immeasurable help in my research.

Some years ago, while going through specimens of annual sunflowers that I had borrowed from several herbaria, I came across a specimen that appeared quite different from the species known to me. It bore the information that it had been collected seven miles west of Fort Stockton, Texas, on September 11, 1947, by H. R. Reed. I found collections of the same plant among the specimens from three different herbaria. At first I thought it might be the rare *H. praetermissus*, but some study convinced me that it was distinct not only from that species but also from any known sunflower. I did not describe it as a species new to science immediately, however, for I hoped to get more material. In 1950, I had a student in my class, Theodore Odell, who lived near Monahans, which is not too far from Fort Stockton. I asked him if he would look for this sunflower when he went home the next summer. He did so and returned with seeds of a sunflower from south of Monahans. I grew it the next year, and when it came into flower I knew immediately that it was not the same as the material from Fort Stockton but that it also was an undescribed species. It was eventually described under the name *H. neglectus*.

The plant from Fort Stockton was not forgotten, however, and on another trip to Arizona I went by way of Texas. I made an intensive effort to find this sunflower, including a detailed search seven miles west of Fort Stockton. There was a marshy area there, and I had previously concluded from a study of the root that this species might grow in wet areas. But there were no sunflowers in bloom. Since it was August and Reed's specimen had been collected in September, I thought that it was too early for it to be in flower, but I found nothing resembling it in the vegetative state. A few dried-up plants of a sunflower were found nearby, and I managed to collect seeds. When I grew them the next year, they gave rise to the common sunflower, as I had suspected they would. After Raymond Jackson made a search of the same area for me two years later and failed to find the plant, I concluded that it was unlikely that we were going to be able to obtain it. I decided to go ahead and publish it as a new species. In 1958, *H. paradoxus* was duly described with a Latin description and appeared in the journal *Rhodora*.

The publication of a new species is ordinarily not a particularly significant or newsworthy event. There is no great honor associated with it. It is simply the duty of the taxonomist to put such things on record. I did not expect to hear any more about it, but I did. Through a former student of mine it came back to me that a well-known Texas taxonomist had said that in all probability it was not a species at all but just another hybrid involving the common sunflower. I was half-inclined to put this down to jealousy; the Texas botanist might think that I was invading his territory. But then I heard that a prominent New York botanist, an outstanding authority on the composite family, thought that perhaps I had been studying sunflowers too long and was losing my judgment about what constituted a species and, moreover, that it was unlike me to describe a new species on the basis of a single collection.

Therefore, I resolved that I would make another search for this species as soon as I could make arrangements. This time I tried later in the year than previously, for the specimen had been collected in September and all our searches had been in August. It was difficult for me to make an extended trip in September since this was the time of the year that I advised students and began teaching. If I could make the trip by air, it would save a lot of time. Accordingly I asked and received permission from the National Science Foundation to use money from my grant for the travel. Although the trip could hardly be justified to search for this one species, it

In 1962 the author's assistant, Alvin Reeves, found it necessary to use a ladder to prepare a giant sunflower for pollination.

would also enable me to get seeds of some of the other late-blooming species of the area. On September 8, 1961, I took a night flight to Midland, Texas, the nearest airport to Fort Stockton. I rented a car and started toward Fort Stockton. Along the way I saw fields of sunflowers, but they were either the common sunflower or *H. petiolaris*. (Over the years I had become expert at identifying the species from a car. I will not say that I can do it for all the species, but I think I can for most of them.) Ten miles north of Fort Stockton I spotted a patch of sunflowers that were obviously some other species. I stopped to examine them. My first impression was that they were *H. paradoxus*, and as I examined them carefully I became convinced of it. There were only some fifty plants in the population, growing in a moist meadow beside a stream. Nearby on drier sites were common sunflowers. I collected a few plants for herbarium specimens, collected buds for chromosome studies, and took photographs. But I could not collect seeds, for the plants were just coming into flower. Perhaps there would be other populations in a more mature stage. I drove on to Fort Stockton and spent the rest of the morning and early afternoon combing the area, including the place where it had been previously collected, but I failed to find a single other plant of *H. paradoxus*.

It was important that I obtain seeds, and I decided that the most likely individual to get them for me would be the local high-school biology teacher. I found the high school and inquired in the principal's office for the biology teacher. In a few minutes I found myself talking to Noel M. Hall. I explained the problem to him, described the place where the sunflower was growing, and asked if he could get seeds for me later in the fall. "No difficulty at all," he assured me, and it turned out that he lived less than a half-mile from where the plants were growing.

A few months later I had the achenes. The next summer the plants were grown, and hybrids were attempted with several species, including the common sunflower and others that I thought were related to *H. paradoxus*. The next year the hybrids were grown, and all of them proved to be nearly sterile, producing few or no good seeds. I was already satisfied that *H. paradoxus* was a "good" species, but the fact that it would not produce fertile hybrids with other species would help to prove my case to any who might still doubt it. Moreover, the hybridizations provided information concerning the relationships of the species.

So far as I am aware, *H. paradoxus* has never been seen in any other place, and I do not know if it still survives in the area near Fort Stockton.

My first sunflower garden was a small plot about ten feet by ten feet in a vacant lot near my parents' home in St. Louis. As I recall, I grew about a half-dozen plants each of the common sunflower and *H. petiolaris* and a few tomatoes (they were not for experimental purposes). I made my first pollinations that summer to secure hybrids, and I still get a feeling of satisfaction whenever I try to make a cross between two species.

Not all of my sunflower work has been in trips and work in the garden. In fact, some of the trips have yielded enough plants and seeds for years of study in the greenhouse and laboratory. I have spent countless hours at the microscope looking at chromosomes and pollen; many more hours measuring leaves, bracts, achenes, and so on; making herbarium specimens, and studying dried specimens. Some of this work has been exciting, but some of it, I must admit, was rather dull and tedious. I find that the beginning student frequently does not realize how many routine tasks are involved in any research program.

It should be obvious by now that I have enjoyed working with sunflowers. This book is a by-product of my studies. During the time that I have been at Indiana University I have been furnished the greenhouse and field space, the microscopes and other equipment that I have needed for research. More important is that for most of that time I have been provided an environment conducive to research. I have been employed there as a professor of botany, and through the years I have taught courses in that subject. At the same time my teaching load has been such that I have had time to do research. In fact, I have been expected to carry on research, as is true of professors at most major universities. My research, however, has never been confined to the school day, but, like that of most researchers, has involved nights, weekends, and holidays. I should perhaps add that my research has not been solely confined to sunflowers but has involved several other plant groups as well.

When I began my research more than twenty-five years ago, I found that there was widespread misunderstanding of the role of the professor-researcher outside the university. Today, I am sorry to say, much misunderstanding is still present. I do not maintain, as some do, that one has to be engaged in research to be a good teacher. But in my case, and probably in that of many others, research involvement has

The author pollinating a sunflower in his garden in 1973.

provided an enthusiasm as well as greater knowledge to make
courses worthwhile and interesting. The research workers are
participating in the work that they are trying to get across to
the students. Their research interest means that they have
to stay up to date in the advances in their field, and hence
they are often better prepared as teachers.

In addition to the generous support of Indiana University,
I have also held grants from the National Science Foundation, which has aided my research by providing funds to
employ part-time student help, to finance my travels, and in
some years, my summer salary as well. Thus it is apparent
that the taxpayers have largely provided the money for my
investigations, and they have every right to ask what my research has contributed. While the research has been enjoyable
for me, that is certainly no justification for using the tax-

payers' money. To justify my work to other scientists and to others in the university to whom I am held accountable is not too difficult, but to give an answer that will satisfy the general public is another matter. I shall try.

Research is usually divided into two main kinds: pure, basic, or fundamental research and applied research. Pure research is an attempt to make new discoveries, and it is curiosity that stimulates the investigator, whereas applied research, such as making a disease-resistant or higher-yielding sunflower, has direct applications to human use or welfare. The latter kind of research usually depends upon the former for the basic knowledge to achieve the practical results. To breed a better sunflower involves putting into application principles of genetics gained from pure research. Without pure research there could be no applied research. Today most pure research is done in the universities, and I would classify my studies of sunflowers as pure research.

While all scientists, I am sure, would be pleased to point to some outstanding discovery resulting from their research, few are able to do so. Science grows largely from the accumulation of many small discoveries. There are, of course, occasional breakthroughs or major achievements on the part of some individuals, although today these breakthroughs are more likely to come from teams than from a single person. It should be obvious that I am building up to the fact that I have made no outstanding discoveries.

Looking back over my more than twenty-five years of research with sunflowers and casting all modesty aside, what can I point to that justifies the support that I have received? Probably my most significant contributions have been those elucidating hybridization and its evolutionary role. In a sense I was in the right place at the right time. Shortly before I had begun my studies, Edgar Anderson had postulated that interspecific hybridization was an important evolutionary phenomenon. He had only limited experimental evidence for his hypotheses, and his ideas met with skepticism among some botanists and zoologists. My work, based not only on the study of hybridization in the field but on the experimental production of hybrids as well, supplied evidence supporting Professor Anderson's claims. My papers on the subject have been widely referred to by other scientists in their studies of hybridization and have served as examples to illustrate hybridization in textbooks.

My studies on the origin of the cultivated sunflower have also been of some general interest. When I began my work, it was thought that the wild common sunflower was the ancestor of the giant cultivated sunflower, for most botanists had long considered them as belonging to the same species. My studies have demonstrated this fairly conclusively. Perhaps of greater importance, not only to botanists but to anthropologists as well, was my hypothesis that the sunflower was first domesticated not in the agricultural centers of Mexico or the Southwest but in the central area of the United States.

Many botanists study plants that have no known use to man, as, for example, certain species of sunflowers, and from the standpoint of pure research one need not study only plants of importance to man. Any research that pushes back the boundaries of the unknown is important. It may have no immediate practical application, and may never have, but frequently we have no way of judging what pure research may be of future benefit to the welfare of mankind.

It so happens that with sunflowers I was working with a plant of direct interest to man. Have my basic studies contributed in any way to producing a "better" sunflower?

My students and I have put on record a lot of information about sunflowers. We have provided keys to identify the species, we have mapped the distributions of all the species, we have determined their chromosome numbers, and we have shown which species can hybridize with each other. Obviously this information can be extremely useful to the plant breeder who is looking to wild sunflowers as the source of disease resistance to incorporate into the cultivated sunflowers, as well as in other ways.

Over the years I have also supplied seeds or rootstocks of many species to plant breeders, both in this country and abroad. In fact, it was the seeds of *H. petiolaris* that I supplied to Patrice Leclercq which enabled him to discover a source of the male sterility that has provided a practical method for the commercial production of sunflower hybrids.

Finally, I would like to point out that the sunflower has provided material for the training of several students, four of whom received Ph.D.'s with dissertations on sunflowers. These students, in turn, have made contributions as teachers and in research.

Bloomington, Indiana   CHARLES B. HEISER, JR.

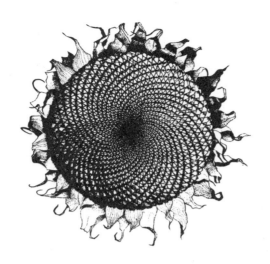

Contents

Illustrations

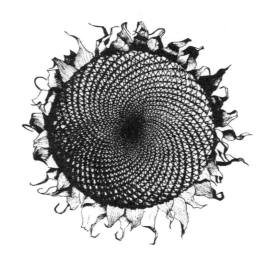

THE SUNFLOWER

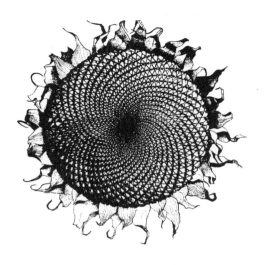

I

Points of View

~~~~~~

NEARLY everyone has seen a sunflower. Wild sunflowers cover thousands of acres in North America, weed sunflowers are common in vacant lots and fields and along roadsides in much of the United States, and giant sunflowers are cultivated around the world. The plants have served man in various ways. The seeds are an important source of food, the flowers have inspired both poet and artist, and red sunflowers have ornamented our gardens.

The story begins in prehistoric times with the American Indian, who found that the seeds of wild sunflowers were a rich source of food and eventually domesticated the plant. In addition to using it for food, the Indians discovered medicinal and other uses for the plant and considered it so important that they paid homage to it in their religious

The common sunflower, state flower of Kansas, and common "weed" throughout much of the United States.

ceremonies. After the discovery of America the sunflower went to Europe, where it excited considerable curiosity because of its size. But it did not come into its own until it reached Russia, where it became a major crop plant. The sunflower, in fact, has become the second-largest oil crop in the world, exceeded only by the soybean.

Today, not too surprisingly, many people think of the sunflower as a Russian plant. While it is true that nowhere in the world is the sunflower more appreciated than in the Soviet Union, it is not totally overlooked in its homeland. It is, as most people know, the state flower of Kansas. We learn about it from the Session Laws of Kansas of June 1, 1903:

WHEREAS, Kansas has a native wild flower common throughout her borders, hardy and conspicuous, of definite, unvarying and striking shape, easily sketched, moulded, and carved, having armorial

The giant single-headed cultivated sunflower.

capacities, ideally adapted for artistic reproduction, with its strong, distinct disk and its golden circle of clear glowing rays—a flower that a child can draw on a slate, a woman can work in silk, or a man can carve on stone or fashion in clay; and

WHEREAS, This flower has to all Kansans a historic symbolism which speaks of frontier days, winding trails, pathless prairies, and is full of life and glory of the past, the pride of the present, and richly emblematic of the majesty of a golden future, and is a flower which has given Kansas the worldwide name, "The Sunflower State": therefore,

Be it enacted by the Legislature of the State of Kansas: That the *Helianthus* or wild native sunflower is hereby made, designated and declared to be the state flower and floral emblem of the State of Kansas.

It was appropriate that the sunflower became the symbol of

the Republicans during the presidential campaign of 1936, when Alfred Landon of Kansas was chosen as their candidate. That not everyone, however, held such lofty opinions of the sunflower as did the Kansans is apparent from this story about the noted botanist, Paul C. Standley, as related by Robert E. Woodson, Jr.:

Back in 1936 I happened to be in Chicago during the heat of the presidential campaign and, during lunch, I asked Standley what were his political preferences. "Just yesterday," he remarked casually, "I did my best for the Republicans." It developed that he had had a visit from a Republican functionary who was in charge of publicity for the campaign of Governor Alf M. Landon of Kansas, the "Sunflower State."

"Doctor Standley," the man explained, "we would like you to give us some facts of general interest about the sunflower which we may use for the support of Governor Landon." "Surely," agreed Standley briskly. "The sunflower is an obnoxious weed; it impoverishes the soil upon which it grows." The man cleared his throat and smiled uneasily. "We'll skip that one, Doctor," he said. "Can you think of some way in which the sunflower might be regarded as a symbol of America's position in world affairs?" "Yes," Standley conceded, "sunflower seeds are the favorite light snack of the Russians." "Oh, no," the man moaned, "try again—possibly something of a parallel of the sunflower and the American people. . . ." "Surely," Standley resumed, "the sunflower is a natural hybrid of uncertain parentage." "Doctor Standley," the sweating man exploded, "Can't you say anything *good* about the sunflower?" "I'm afraid not," was the smug reply. "You see, I'm a Democrat."

Somewhat less than kind feelings toward sunflowers were also expressed by the Iowa legislature in 1969. Since the sunflower is a serious weed among crops, particularly soybeans, in parts of Iowa, a measure was introduced to have the sunflower declared a noxious weed. If the law had been enacted, it would have meant that county weed commissioners could force eradication of the plant. The matter was treated with

Joan Wood examines a Mammoth Russian sunflower; ornamental varieties are in the background.

Sunflowers can be a nuisance to a farmer when he is trying to harvest corn, even in Kansas! Courtesy of the *Topeka Capital-Journal*.

proper decorum before the house, where one representative asked his fellows, "Have you no love of beauty in your souls?" Another representative was concerned with the reaction in their sister state, fearing that Kansas might make reprisals.

He was correct, for in no time at all the Kansas legislature retaliated by introducing a resolution declaring the eastern goldfinch, the state bird of Iowa, a public nuisance. The resolution went on to declare the goldfinch an unattractive, bothersome, and raucously noisy creature that served no useful purpose on God's green earth. The governor of Iowa offered a solution to the "flower-feather fracas," as it was referred to by the press, when he offered to exchange all of Iowa's sunflowers for Kansas' supply of goldfinches. Neither resolution was ever formally adopted, and relations between the two states have more or less returned to normal.

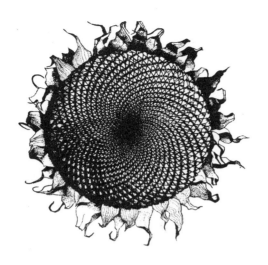

II

The Sunflower of the Botanist

THERE ARE sixty-seven kinds or species of sunflowers, some of them with many varieties or races. Most of the species are confined to North America and grow in various habitats from deserts to marshy areas and from sea level to over seven thousand feet. A dozen or so species are found only in the Andes of South America; some of them are still poorly studied because they grow in rather inaccessible places at high altitudes. The sunflowers are known scientifically by the genus name *Helianthus*, from the Greek *helios*, meaning "sun," and *anthos*, meaning "flower." The sunflower that is best known the world over is *Helianthus annuus* L., the "common sunflower" or just plain "sunflower" to Kansans and to millions of other people. This species of sunflower is extremely variable and includes branched forms with rather small flower

11

12

heads which are common in the wild, particularly in western North America; unbranched forms with massive flower heads which are cultivated for their oily seeds; and still others with red or double flowers which are grown for their ornamental value. Throughout this book when the word "sunflower" is used alone, it refers to this species.

The "L." following *Helianthus annuus* stands for Linnaeus, the great Swedish naturalist, who in the eighteenth century gave this plant and thousands of others their Latin names. Linnaeus was very much pleased with his choice of a name for the sunflower plant, as is attested to by his account: "Who can see this plant in flower, whose great golden blossoms send out rays in every direction from the circular disk, without admiring the handsome flower modelled on the Sun's shape? And as one admires, presently the name occurs to the mind, even as, if one sees only the name, the admired picture of the flower comes before one." At the time it was named, it was the only sunflower known to Linnaeus that lived a single season, hence it was called *annuus*, for "annual." Today a dozen other annual species of sunflowers are recognized. The rest of the sunflowers are perennials, some of which are cultivated as ornamentals, and one of which has achieved some fame as a food plant and is known as Jerusalem artichoke—although it is neither from Jerusalem nor an artichoke. The South American species are mostly shrubs, some of them in fact being almost small trees.

The sunflowers are related to the daisies, asters, marigolds, dandelions, and black-eyed Susans, all of which are members of the family of plants known as the Compositae, which, next to the orchids, is the largest family of flowering plants and one of the most highly developed from an evolutionary standpoint. In spite of its large size the family has supplied mankind very few food plants; the sunflower is one kind of food, and lettuce, artichokes, salsify, and chicory are others. The

The western variety of the common sunflower, originally described as a distinct species (*Helianthus lenticularis*). *Botanical Register*, Vol. XV (1829).

family more than makes up for this failure, however, by furnishing a large number of showy flowers for our gardens. It has also produced some obnoxious weeds—ragweed is one of the most notorious.

Obviously all these plants have certain characters in common that place them in the same botanical family. One of the important characters that holds them together as a group is that a sunflower or a daisy is not a single flower at all, but a whole bouquet. If one examines a sunflower closely, he will find that there are many—perhaps a hundred or more—small flowers packed together in a structure known as a head.[1] In 1636 the herbalist John Gerard described the arrangement of flowers "as though a cunning workeman had of purpose placed them in very good order, much like the honie combes of bees."

On the outside of the head is a series of greenish bracts. One who knows a little about flowers might regard them as sepals, but actually they are phyllaries, or little leaves. Next to the phyllaries are found the ray flowers, usually yellow in the sunflower and white in the daisy. When one plays "She loves me, she loves me not" with a daisy, he will be pulling off these flowers, which the uninitiated may refer to as petals. Although normally flowers serve to produce seeds, the ray flowers of the sunflower are sterile, and apparently their sole function is to attract insects. This specialization of flower structure is another reason for considering this composite flower a highly evolved type.

The flowers in the center of the head, called disk flowers, are smaller and quite different in shape from the ray flowers and sometimes even of a different color. If one examines one of the disk flowers closely, he will find a tubular five-lobed corolla which represents five fused petals. Below the corolla is the inferior ovary—so called because of its position. On

---

[1] The idea that the sunflower is highly evolved because it knew how to get ahead is not given serious consideration by most botanists!

Details of the head of a sunflower. Drawing by Joan Wood.

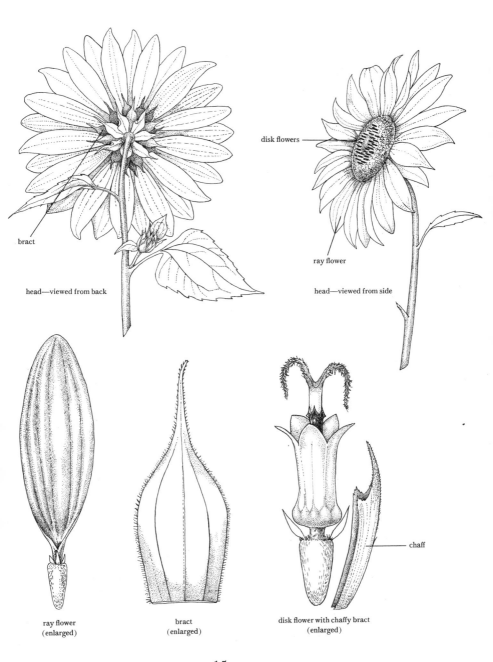

bract

head—viewed from back

disk flowers

ray flower

head—viewed from side

ray flower
(enlarged)

bract
(enlarged)

chaff

disk flower with chaffy bract
(enlarged)

15

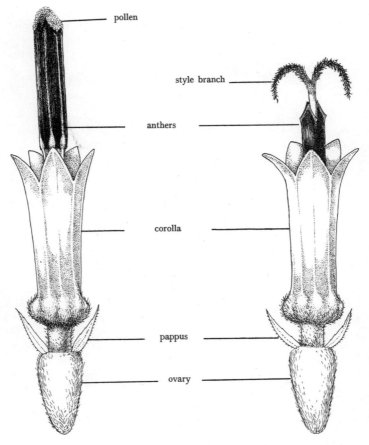

Disk flowers of the sunflower: flowers with pollen (*left*); flowers with style branches opened (*right*). Drawing by Joan Wood.

either side on the top of the ovary are two small scalelike structures, technically known as the pappi, which are thought to represent the sepals. In many composites the pappi provide for efficient dispersal of the fruit. Anyone who has blown on a dandelion or pulled Spanish needles from his trousers has seen how the pappus operates. In the one it has been modified into a parachutelike device to allow fruit dissemination by

Close-up of portion of sunflower showing (*left to right*) rays, disk flowers with style branches exposed, disk flowers presenting pollen, and unopened disk-flower buds.

wind, and in the other the barbed pappus awns are a specialization for the fruit to gain a free ride on passing animals. In the sunflower, however, the pappus has no apparent function and falls off as the fruit matures. The sunflower, although it has no special means of seed dispersal, still manages to get around very well, as we shall shortly see.

Let us return to the disk flowers for a closer examination. These flowers are "perfect"—to use the word in its botanical sense to mean that they contain both male and female producing parts. In order for reproduction to take place, the pollen (which will produce the sperm) has to come into contact with the stigma of the pistil (which contains the ovule with the egg). Fertilization resulting from the crossing of different plants frequently has certain desirable results, and the sunflower and its relatives have evolved a remarkable method of ensuring such outbreeding.

17

Sunflower head after pollination. The withered disk flowers are seated on top of the achenes. Bracts are on the left.

The pollen-producing structures (the anthers) form a tube around the style of the pistil. The pollen is shed to the inside of this tube, and as the style grows, it pushes the pollen out the top. The pollen is then ready to be picked up by any insects that happen to visit the flower in search of pollen or nectar. Once the style has pushed the pollen out by its piston-like action, it splits open, exposing the stigmatic surface, which thus far has remained virgin but is now ready to receive pollen. Although bees are the most common visitors, almost any insect that brushes against the stigma or walks over it may leave pollen, which very well could come from another plant and thus bring about cross-pollination. The pollen grows down the style, and in a short time sperms are discharged, one of which will fuse with the egg and thereby initiate the development of a new seed. If by chance, however, the flower does not receive pollen from an outside source, the stigma curves around and eventually contacts its own pollen so that self-pollination may then take place, thus ensuring seed set. Although self-pollination does occur in many composites in

Arrangement of achenes in the head, "much like the honie combes of bees."

this manner, it rarely does in sunflowers, for pollen of any given sunflower will seldom germinate on the stigma of the same plant, a phenomenon that is known as self-incompatibility. Thus cross-pollination is obligatory if seed is to set.

The whole intricate arrangement of the head and the structure of the flowers can be explained largely as an adaptation to bring about pollination, which, along with food making, seed dispersal, and germination, constitute the most important events in the life of any plant. Not only the sunflower but probably all flower structure can be explained as some sort of adaptation for pollination by wind, water, or animals. The sunflower and other composites have become marvelously adapted to pollination by insects. They have by no means reached the ultimate in devices for pollination—orchids, for example, have achieved far more elaborate methods. Although most orchids are adapted to attract insects searching for nectar, certain species have evolved in such a way that the flowers resemble the females of certain wasps. The male of the species is hence attracted to the flower in a search for

19

A fairly large sunflower head. Completely dry, it measured four-teen inches in diameter.

something other than food, and in attempting to copulate with the flower he brings about pollination—certainly one of nature's unique methods of pollination.

Although flowers and bees are sometimes used to teach children the so-called facts of life, it can be seen from the foregoing account that the sex life of plants is not a simple affair. The events following the union of the sperm and egg are perhaps even more complicated than the preceding but do not require elucidation here. For the present account it is sufficient to point out that in the sunflower the matured ovary or fruit, which, botanically speaking, is an achene, contains a single seed. In common language the fruit is often called a seed, while in reality the seed is only the part that is eaten, and the hull, or the seed coat, is part of the ovary rather than a true seed coat. The same mistake is made when one speaks of a grain of corn as a seed; the grain is the fruit that contains a seed.

Although the details of the sexual behavior of the sunflower are important to the botanist, the nonbotanical reader has by now perhaps learned more than he cares to know about the subject. The size of sunflowers, while not an unusually important scientific matter, may be of more general interest. Witness the newspapers across the nation which at the end of each summer run a photograph of a sunflower grown by Mr. So and So that reached a height of so many feet with a "flower" (head) so wide. The tallest sunflower ever reported is from an account in the sixteenth century of plants reaching heights of twenty-four feet. Although one may be justly skeptical of this report, there are reliable records of forms of the common sunflower reaching eighteen feet, which is not bad for a single season's growth. Recent exact records on the size of the head are easily available, for during the past several years the magazine *Organic Gardening* has held a contest for the largest sunflower. The record to date, as far as I have been able to learn, is two and one-half feet, truly a gigantic sunflower. Heads one foot across are more common. Data on the length of the achenes ("seeds") are readily available since thousands have been measured in connection with various scientific studies. The average giant sunflower has an achene about a half-inch long, and one variety from Turkey is known to have achenes over an inch in length. Some nearly as long have been found in archaeological deposits in North Dakota. The current trend in commercial sunflowers has been away from the tall plants with giant heads and large achenes, for harvesting of smaller sorts is much more readily accomplished.

After commenting on its size, people frequently ask whether the sunflower really follows the sun. The Spanish name for the plant, *girasol*, and the French name, *tournesol*, literally mean "turn with the sun." Let us postpone the answer until we have heard from the poets in the next chapter.

21

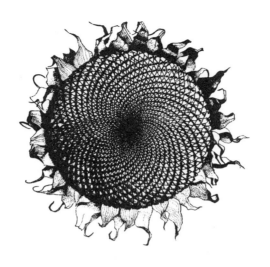

III

The Sunflower of the Poet

FLOWERS have always appealed to artist and poet alike, and the sunflower has been no exception. It has served as a model for both the beginning and the professional artist and has been depicted in a great variety of styles from the modernistic interpretations of Diego Rivera to the classical of Van Gogh, Renoir, Monet, and Gauguin. There is even a painting of *Van Gogh Painting Sunflowers* by Gauguin. It is the poet, however, who concerns us here. No aspect of the plant has more inspired the poet than the sunflower's supposed turning with the sun. The sunflower's "love" for the sun has been expressed in many different ways.

In his *Arcadia*, of 1590, Sir Philip Sidney wrote:

With gazing looks, short sighs, unsettled feet,
He stood, but turn'd, as Girosol to sunne;
His fancies still did her in halfe-way meet,
His soule did flie as she was seene to run.

The "Girosol" may represent the sunflower. If so this would be the earliest poetic reference to the plant. There can be little question about the identity of the plant involved in Abraham Cowley's poem a half-century later, for it is entitled "Of Plants: The Sunflower":

I still adore my Sire with prostrate Face,
Turn where he turns, and all his motions trace.

The sunflower is represented as masculine, and nearly all subsequent poets, with the exception of Thomas Moore, followed Cowley's lead in this regard. Botanically speaking, the plant is neither male nor female, but this need not trouble the poet.

In the early part of the eighteenth century James Thomson became the first English poet of note to pay his respects to the sunflower. His interpretation of the anatomy of the plant is somewhat different from that of the botanist, however; the ray flowers become "leaves" and the head a "bosom." From *The Seasons*, "Summer":

But one, the lofty follower of the sun
Sad when he sets, shuts up her yellow leaves,
Drooping all night; and, when he warm returns
Points her enamour'd bosom to his ray.

Although Erasmus Darwin (whose greatest claim to fame is that he was the grandfather of Charles) is not fully accepted by either the scientists or the poets, he wrote in couplets and thus deserves inclusion here. In his "The Botanic Garden, Love of the Plants," he wrote of the sunflower:

With zealous step he climbs the upland lawn,
And bows in homage to rising dawn;
Imbibes with eagle eye the golden ray
And watches, as it moves, the orb of day.

Young giant sunflowers viewed from the west at 7:00 P.M.

One of the best-known sunflower poems, and deservedly so, is from William Blake's *Songs of Experience*, of 1794:

> *Ah, sunflower! weary of time*
> *Who countest the steps of the sun*
> *Seeking after that sweet golden clime*
> *Where the traveler's journey is done.*

Percy Bysshe Shelley's contribution to the sunflower tradition comes from his translation of Calderón's *El Mágico prodigioso*:

> *Light-enchanted sunflower, thou*
> *Who gazest ever true and tender*
> *On the sun's revolving splendour.*

The original has it thusly:

> *Aquel girasol, que está*
> *viendo cara á cara al sol*
> *Tras cuyo hermoso arrebol*
> *siempre moviendose va.*

The British poet and journalist James Montgomery does not state unequivocally that the sunflower turns with the sun, but certainly he belongs in this account, for he used "The Sun-Flower" for his title:

> *Eagle of flowers! I see thee stand,*
> *   And on the sun's noon-glory gaze;*
> *With eyes like his, thy lids expand,*
> *   And fringe their disk with golden rays;*
> *Though fix'd on earth, in darkness rooted there,*
> *   Light is thine element, thy dwelling air,*
> *   Thy prospect heaven.*

Thomas Moore left little doubt about the sunflower's movements in the second verse of his "Believe Me, If All Those Endearing Young Charms":

> *No, the heart that has truly lov'd never forgets*
> *But as truly loves on to the close:*
> *As the sunflower turns on her god, when he sets*
> *The same look she turn'd when he rose.*

By all odds the longest sunflower poem, Charles Swinburne's "The Complaint of Lisa," is not really about sunflowers at all. It is based upon the Tenth Day of Novel 7 of the *Decameron* of Giovanni Boccaccio, which tells the story of Lisa, a commoner, who falls in love with a king at first sight. Realizing that she has no chance of having her love returned, she becomes ill and is near death. When the king learns of this, he visits her and gives her one kiss. From that day on the king is Lisa's knight. Swinburne chose the sunflower as the symbol for the knight:

Wild sunflower viewed from the south at 7:00 P.M.

There is not one upon life's weariest way
Who is weary as I am weary of all but death.
Toward whom I look as looks the sunflower
All day with his whole soul toward the sun. . . .

Aye, all day long he has no eye for me:
With golden eye following the golden sun
From rose-coloured to purple-pillowed bed,
From birthplace to the flame-lit place of death
From eastern end to western of his way,
So mine eye follows thee, my sunflower.

A few more recent writers have also contributed, among them Clinton Scollard. This from his "Sunflowers":

Still my sunflowers love the sun;
Keep their ward and watch and wait
Till the rosy key of morning
Opens the Eastern Gate.

This, from Robert P. Tristram Coffin's poem, also entitled "Sunflowers":

> *The dials of these honeyed clocks*
> *Fringed with leaves of sun*
> *Turn obedient to the wheels*
> *That make the daystar run.*

And this, from Nora S. Unwin's "Giant Sunflowers":

> *The garden king returns*
> *With broad and golden gaze*
> *The sun's brave stare.*

What can the botanist say about the turning of the sunflower to the sun, in view of the overwhelming evidence from the poets? He can say, "Not so." This opinion was expressed in the 1690's by the English herbalist John Gerard: "The flour of the Sun is called in Latine *Flos Solis*, for that some have reported it to turn with the Sun, which I could never observe, although I have endeavored to finde out the truth of it; but I rather thinke it was so called because it resembles the radiant beams of the Sunne."

The facts are: green plants are phototropic and respond by growing toward the source of light. Thus many plants, particularly at early stages, bend toward the east in the morning and toward the west in the evening. The common sunflower shows this tendency more strikingly than most plants, but, once the flower head opens, it no longer bends toward the source of light. Interestingly enough, in my gardens the heads of the giant sunflowers always end up facing the east. I have no explanation for this, but the poet would tell us that the plant is awaiting the return of its god, the sun.

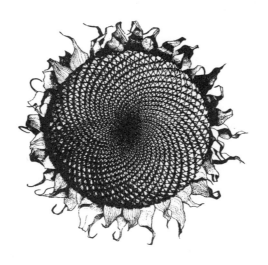

IV

The Sunflower Among the
North American Indians

*This young man talked to me out among
the sunflowers and I did not answer him.
Now he has gone to war and is killed.*
                                    —From a Mandan Indian song

ALTHOUGH he has left us no written record of it, the American Indian was the first to see and to appreciate the sunflower. The archaeologist has found remains of his plants that in many ways tell us more than words alone. In spite of the fact that plant remains are rarely preserved because of their perishable nature, some have withstood the ravages of time so that we have some idea what the first Americans ate in the days of prehistory. Our knowledge of their first foods advanced slowly because the vegetable remains are not as spectacular as their pottery and their weapons and were therefore largely ignored by the early archaeologists. Chief among the food remains is corn—an ear of corn if kept dry will last almost forever, and bushels of corn have been turned up in archaeological excavations in the Americas. Various types of beans and squash were other basic foods of the North American Indian. Sunflowers and other food plants are less frequently discovered, but sunflower achenes, which are of durable construction, have now been found at several archaeological sites in the United States.

The second source of our information concerning the Indians' appreciation of the sunflower comes from the notebooks and journals of the early explorers. These explorers, such as Champlain, Lewis and Clark, Prince Maximilian of Wied, and Paul Wilhelm, Duke of Württemberg, made meticulous notes on the customs of the Indians, and fortunately the food plants were not beneath their notice. In some regions the explorers found primitive Indians gathering wild sunflower achenes for food, and in other regions they actually saw the plants being cultivated along with corn and beans.

The earliest inhabitants of America did not practice agriculture and had to depend upon wild plants for their vegetable food. The sunflowers—if they grew as they do today—covered thousands of square miles in what is now the western United States and furnished an abundance of seeds for food. Many groups of western Indians never reached the agricultural stage, and the early explorers of the West found the native tribes still gathering seeds much as their ancestors had done thousands of years earlier.

We have several excellent accounts of the gathering and preparation of the seeds of the wild sunflower. John Wesley Powell's description of the seed harvesting by the Shivwits (a Paiute tribe) in the Grand Canyon region is one of the most nearly complete:

> They gather the seeds of many plants, as sunflowers, golden rods, and grasses. For this purpose they have large conical baskets, which hold two or more bushels. The women carry them by their backs, suspended from their foreheads by broad straps, and with a smaller one in the left hand, and a willow woven fan in the right, they walk

among the grasses, and sweep the seed into a smaller basket, which is emptied, now and then, into a larger, until it is full of seeds and chaff; then they winnow out the chaff and roast the seeds. They roast these curiously; they put the seeds, with a quantity of red hot coals, into a willow tray, and, by rapidly and dexterously shaking and tossing them, keep the coals aglow, and the seeds and tray from burning. As if by magic, so skilled are the crones in this work, they roll the seeds to one side of the tray, as they are roasted, and the coals to the other. Then they grind the seeds into a fine flour, and make it into cakes and mush.

In another region Lewis and Clark observed that the "seeds" were pounded and rubbed between smooth stones to make a meal which was a favorite among the Indians. Among the Zuñis of the Southwest, who also cultivated the giant sunflower, the wild sunflower seeds were gathered and "shucked by being reheated in the roasting tray" and then "rolled lightly under the muller and the oily meats [the seeds] came out clean." An old Apache is credited with saying that there was food everywhere if one knew how to find it: "You see that big field of sunflowers; well, they contain much food, for we take the seeds, reduce them to flour upon our matates and make it into cakes which are very nice." Sunflower cakes were taken on war forays, and according to one observer sustained the warrior against fatigue better than any other food.

Wild sunflowers have been found at only a few archaeological sites—a single achene has been found in Colorado, and a fairly large deposit of heads of not only the common sunflower but of two other species as well has been found at Tularosa Cave and other sites in New Mexico. The New Mexican Indians did not depend entirely upon wild plants for food, for remains of corn, squash, and beans, all of which must have been cultivated, were recovered at the same site. It is, of course, possible that the sunflowers were also cultivated, but it seems more likely that the seeds came from wild plants which grew in the vicinity. The fact that these Indians had cultivated plants but still collected wild sunflowers perhaps indicates the esteem in which they held the sunflower.

The wild sunflowers were also utilized in other ways. Many

wild plants have been used as medicine at one time or another, and the sunflower is no exception. The Zuñis used it as a cure for rattlesnake bites. Among the Dakotas an infusion made from sunflower heads was used to relieve chest pains, and other tribes in widely separated regions are also reported to have employed them to soothe the chest. Among the Pawnees the seeds were pounded with certain roots and taken in dry form by pregnant women so that later their nursing babies would not become sick. In 1952, Charles H. Lange, an anthropologist at the University of Texas, wrote me that "among the Cochiti, a reliable 'home remedy' for cuts and other wounds is the juice of freshly crushed sunflower stems. The juice is smeared liberally over the wounds, bandaged, and invariably results in a speedy recovery—with never a case of infection." Others have mentioned that the sunflower itself furnished the bandage. The sticky, resinous juice of the stem was spread over the wound and hardened to form a dressing. The medicinal use of sunflowers was to be taken up by Europeans, as we shall learn in a later chapter.

Plants that are important to primitive man nearly always become associated with his religious and social customs. The wild sunflower was worn in the hair of Hopi Indians of Arizona during various ceremonies, and carved wooden sunflower disks found at a prehistoric site in Arizona almost certainly were employed in ceremonial rituals in some way. Sunflowers have become involved in the myths of the Indians, and designs of the flowers have been incorporated in their pottery. The sunflower, along with corn, beans, and squash, is mentioned in the creation myth of the Onondagas of New York.

The giant cultivated sunflower plant was even more important to many tribes of Indians than were the wild ones. The giant sunflower, although it cannot grow wild, must have been a particular blessing to the Indian, for in addition to

The Towne of Secota, an Indian village in North Carolina, from the drawing by John White. The sunflowers (E) were not in the original drawing but were added later.

TB   20

having the same uses as the wild plant, it was a better food source because of its much larger seed. Archaeological finds of cultivated sunflowers are reported from several localities in central and northeastern North America. Sometimes the remains consist of only two or three charred achenes, but at one site in Ohio several quarts of achenes have been recovered. Sunflower heads have been found in Kentucky and Ohio. From a comparison of some of these sunflowers with varieties grown today, it is clear that Indians were growing plants in no way inferior to modern varieties in size. Achenes fully an inch long have been found in North Dakota, and very few modern varieties have achenes that even approach this length. Although cultivated sunflowers have not been found by archaeologists in the Southwest, we have several early accounts of the sunflower from this region, and it is clear that the cultivated sunflower must have been widely distributed throughout North America when Europeans first came.

The primary use of the plant originally was probably for food. Thomas Hariot in 1588 wrote of the plants of the Algonquian Indians of the Pamlico Sound region of North Carolina: "There is also another great herbe . . . about sixe foote in height; the head . . . is a spanne in bredth," and it was used for making both a "bread and broth." Among the Choctaw Indians the sunflower meal was mixed with maize flour, "to make a very palatable bread."

The cultivated sunflower was also highly valued for the oil that could be extracted from the seeds, and Iroquoian tribes used it in great quantities. The achenes were bruised in a mortar, and the pounded mass was heated for half an hour and thrown into boiling water until the oil was separated. The water was then cooled and strained, and the oil was skimmed off. The oil was used to season food, to anoint the hair, and to serve as a base for pigments which were painted on the skin during special rituals.

The sunflowers themselves furnished a source of some pigments. A yellow dye was extracted from the ray flowers among a number of tribes, and the Hopi Indians who grew a variety with deep purple achenes obtained a purple dye by soaking

The sunflower of the Hopi Indians of Arizona.

them in water. The dye was used to color basketry or to decorate their bodies. In fact, the use of the sunflower as a source of purple dye may have become more important among the Hopis than its use as a food. The Hopis also used the stems of the cultivated sunflower in the construction of smoke hoods over their baking stones. I was told by a Hopi that the children used to delight in stealing a few achenes to eat when their parents were not looking.

The cultivated sunflower, like its wild relative, reached its southernmost limit in northern Mexico. There the sunflower is sometimes called *maíz tejas* or *maíz de teja,* and some people have used this name as evidence that the sunflower went south from Texas (the Spanish word for which is *Tejas*) and arrived after these Indians had maize (corn). This interpretation may be correct, in regard to the latter part, but the *teja* (Spanish for "tile") probably refers to the tilelike arrangement of the sunflower achenes in the head rather than to the geographic source of the plant. From an early Spanish account of Francisco Hernández we know that the sunflower was used for food in Mexico and had reputed medicinal value in soothing chest pains, but he recorded that when the sunflower was eaten in abundance it caused a headache. He is also perhaps the only writer who ever ascribed aphrodisiac powers to the sunflower.

One of the best, and by far the most nearly complete, accounts of the use of the sunflower is that given by Gilbert L. Wilson in his *Agriculture of the Hidatsa Indians* in 1917. Wilson spent several years studying the agriculture of the Indians on the Fort Berthold Indian Reservation and ultimately submitted the account as his doctoral thesis at the University of Minnesota. His method consisted of interviewing the Indians in regard to the cultivation and use of the plants and is particularly valuable because he presented the remarks of the Indians in full and in their own words insofar as translation allowed. This little-known, very important account deserves quoting in full. Maxi'diwiac, a woman of the Hidatsa tribe, speaks:

This that I am going to tell you of the planting and harvesting of our crops is out of my own experience, seen with my own eyes. In olden times, I know, my tribe used digging sticks and bone hoes for garden tools; and I have described how I saw my grandmother use them. There may be other tools or garden customs once in use in my tribe, and now forgotten; of them I cannot speak. There were families in Like-a-fishhook village less industrious than ours, and some families may have tilled their fields in ways a little different; of them, also, I cannot speak. This that I now tell is as I saw my mothers do, or did myself, when I was young. My mothers were industrious women, and our family had always good crops, and I will tell now how the women of my father's family cared for their fields, as I saw them, and helped them.

The first seed that we planted in the spring was sunflower seed. Ice breaks on the Missouri about the first week in April; and we planted sunflower seed as soon after as the soil could be worked.

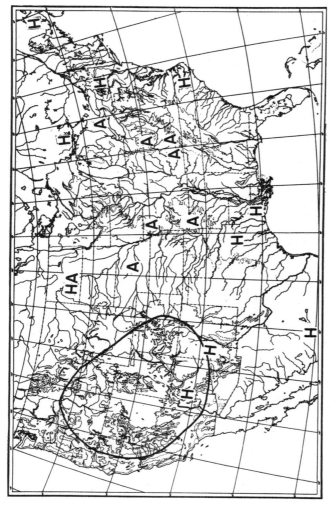

The principal sites where archaeological sunflowers have been found are indicated at A; historical records of sunflower cultivation among the Indians are shown by H; the circled area in the West indicates the area where wild sunflower seeds were gathered by Indians.

Our native name for the lunar month that corresponds most nearly to April, is Mapi-o'ce-mi'di, or Sunflower-planting-moon.

Planting was done by hoe, or the woman scooped up the soil with her hands. Three seeds were planted in a hill, at the depth of the second joint of the woman's finger. The three seeds were planted together, pressed into the loose soil by a single motion, with thumb and first two fingers. The hill was heaped up and patted firm with the palm in the same way as we did for corn.

Usually we planted sunflowers only around the edges of a field. The hills were placed eight or nine paces apart; for we never sowed sunflowers thickly. We thought a field surrounded thus by a sparse-sown row of sunflowers, had a handsome appearance.

Of cultivated sunflowers we had several varieties, black, white, red, striped, named from the color of the seed. The varieties differed only in color; all had the same taste and smell, and were treated alike in cooking.

White sunflower seed when pounded into meal, turned dark, but I think this was caused by the parching.

Each family raised the variety they preferred. The varieties were well fixed; black seed produced black; white seed, white.

Although our sunflower seed was the first crop to be planted in the spring, it was the last to be harvested in the fall.

For harvesting, we reckoned two kinds of flowers, or heads.

A stalk springing from seed of one of our cultivated varieties had one, sometimes two, or even three larger heads,[1] heavy and full, bending the top of the stalk with their weight of seed. Some of these big heads had each a seed area as much as eleven inches across; and yielded each an even double handful of seed. We called the seed from these big heads mapi'-i'-ti'a from mapi', sunflower, or sunflower seed, and i'ti'a, big.

Besides these larger heads, there were other and smaller heads on the stalk; and wild sunflowers bearing similar small heads grew in many places along the Missouri, and were sure to be found

[1] This account of cultivated sunflowers with several heads is of particular interest in that the cultivated sunflower usually has but a single massive head. However, it is known that hybrids between cultivated and wild sunflowers produce several heads, and, in view of the fact that wild sunflowers were common in this area, it is possible that the cultivated sunflowers of these Indians had been contaminated by crossing with the wild types in spite of the fact that she mentions that the varieties were well fixed, white seed producing white, and so on.

springing up in abandoned gardens. These smaller heads of the cultivated, and the heads of the wild plants, were never more than five inches across; and these and their seed we called mapi'-na'ka, sunflower's child or baby sunflower.

Our sunflowers were ready for harvesting when the little petals that covered the seeds fell off, exposing the ripe seeds beneath. Also, the back of the head turned yellow; earlier in the season it would be green.

To harvest the larger heads, I put a basket on my back, and knife in hand, passed from plant to plant, cutting off each large head close to the stem; the severed heads I tossed into my basket. These heads I did not let dry on the stalk, as birds would devour the seeds.

My basket filled, I returned to the lodge, climbed the ladder to the roof, and spread the sunflower heads upon the flat part of the roof around the smoke hole, to dry. The heads were laid face downward, with the backs to the sun. When I was a girl, only three or four earth lodges in the village had peaked roofs; and these lodges were rather small. All the larger and better lodges, those of what we deemed wealthier families, were built with the top of the roof flat, like a floor. A flat roof was useful to dry things on; and when the weather was fair, the men often sat there and gossiped.

The sunflower heads were dried face downward, that the sun falling on the back of the head might dry and shrink the fiber, thus loosening the seeds. The heads were laid flat on the bare roof, without skins or other protection beneath. If a storm threatened, the unthreshed heads were gathered up and borne into the lodge; but they were left on the roof overnight, if the weather was fair.

When the heads had dried about four days, the seeds were threshed out; and I would fetch in from the garden another supply of heads to dry and thresh.

To thresh the heads, a skin was spread and the heads laid on it face downward, and beaten with a stick. Threshing might be on the ground, or on the flat roof, as might be convenient.

An average threshing filled a good sized basket, with enough seed left over to make a small package.

The smaller heads of the cultivated plants were sometimes gathered, dried, and threshed, as were the larger heads; but if the season was getting late and frost had fallen, and the seeds were getting loose in their pods, I more often threshed these smaller heads and those of the wild plants directly from the stalk.

For this I bore a carrying basket, swinging it around over my breast instead of my back; and going about the garden or into the places where the wild plants grew, I held the basket under these smaller, or baby sunflower heads, and beating them smartly with a stick, threshed the seeds into the basket. It took me about half a day to thresh a basket half full. The seeds I took home to dry, before sacking them.

The seeds from the baby sunflowers of both wild and cultivated plants were sacked together. The seeds of the large heads were sacked separately; and in the spring, when we came to plant, our seed was always taken from the sack containing the harvest of the larger heads.

In my father's family, we usually stored away two, sometimes three, sacks of dried sunflower seed for winter use. Sacks were made of skins, perhaps fourteen inches high and eight inches in diameter, on an average.

Sunflower harvest came after we had threshed our corn; and corn threshing was in the first part of October.

Because they were gathered later, the seeds of baby sunflowers were looked upon as a kind of second crop; and as I have said, they were kept apart from the earlier harvest, because seed for planting was selected from the larger and earlier gathered heads. Gathered thus late, this second crop was nearly always touched by the frost, even before the seeds were threshed from the stalks.

This frosting of the seeds had an effect upon them that we rather esteemed. We made a kind of oily meal from sunflower seed, by pounding them in a corn mortar; but meal made from seed that had been frosted, seemed more oily than that from seed gathered before the frost fell. The freezing of the seeds seemed to bring the oil out of the crushed kernels.

This was well known to us. The large heads, left on the roof over night, were sometimes caught by the frost; and meal made from their seed was more oily than that from unfrosted seed. Sometimes we took the threshed seed out of doors and let it get frosted, so as to bring out this oiliness. Frosting the seeds did not kill them.

The oiliness brought out by the frosting was more apparent in the seeds of baby sunflowers than in seeds of the larger heads. Seeds of the latter seemed never to have as much oil in them as seeds of the baby sunflowers.

To make sunflower meal the seeds were first roasted, or parched. This was done in a clay pot, for iron pots were scarce in my tribe when I was young. The clay pot in use in my father's family was about a foot high and eight or nine inches in diameter, as you see from measurements I make with my hands.

This pot I set on the lodge fire, working it down into the coals with a rocking motion, and raked coals around it; the mouth I tipped slightly toward me. I threw into the pot two or three double-handfuls of the seeds and as they parched, I stirred them with a little stick, to keep them from burning. Now and then I took out a seed and bit it; if the kernel was soft and gummy, I knew the parching was not done; but when it bit dry and crisp, I knew the seeds were cooked and I dipped them out with a horn spoon into a wooden bowl. . . .

Again I threw into the pot two or three double-handfuls of seed to parch; and so, until I had enough.

As the pot grew quite hot I was careful not to touch it with my hands. The parching done, I lifted the pot out, first throwing over it a piece of old tent cover to protect my two hands.

Parching the seeds caused them to crack open somewhat.

The parched seeds were pounded in the corn mortar to make meal. Pounding sunflower seeds took longer, and was harder work, than pounding corn.

Sunflower meal was used in making a dish that we called do'patsamakihi'ke, or four-vegetables-mixed; from do'patsa, four things; and makihi'ke, mixed or put together. Four-vegetables-mixed we thought our very best dish.

To make this dish, enough for a family of five, I did as follows:

I put a clay pot with water on the fire.

Into the pot I threw one double-handful of beans. This was a fixed quantity; I put in just one double-handful whether the family to be served was large or small; for a larger quantity of beans in this dish was apt to make gas on one's stomach.

When we dried squash in the fall we strung the slices upon strings of twisted grass, each seven Indian fathoms long; an Indian fathom is the distance between a woman's two hands outstretched on either side. From one of these seven-fathom strings I cut a piece as long as from my elbow to the tip of my thumb; the ends of the severed piece I tied together, making a ring; and this I dropped into the pot with the beans.

When the squash slices were well cooked I lifted them out of the pot by the grass string into a wooden bowl. With a horn spoon I chopped and mashed the cooked squash slices into a mass, which

I now returned to the pot with the beans. The grass string I threw away.

To the mess I now added four or five double-handfuls of mixed meal, of pounded parched sunflower seed and pounded parched corn. The whole was boiled for a few minutes more, and was ready for serving.

I have already told how we parched sunflower seed; and that I used two or three double-handfuls of seed to a parching. I used two parchings of sunflower seed for one mess of four-vegetables-mixed. I also used two parchings of corn; but I put more corn into the pot at a parching than I did of sunflower seed.

Pounding the parched corn and sunflower seed reduced their bulk so that the four parchings, two of sunflower seed and two of corn, made but four or five handfuls of the mixed meals.

Four-vegetables-mixed was eaten freshly cooked; and the mixed corn-and-sunflower meal was made fresh for it each time. A little alkali salt might be added for seasoning, but even this was not usual. No other seasoning was used. Meat was not boiled with the mess, as the sunflower seed gave sufficient oil to furnish fat.

Four-vegetables-mixed was a winter food; and the squash used in its making was dried, sliced squash, never green, fresh squash.

The clay pot used for boiling this and other dishes was about the size of an iron dinner pot, or even larger. For a large family, the pot might be as much as thirteen or fourteen inches high. I have described that in use in my father's family.

When a mess of four-vegetables-mixed was cooked, I did not remove the pot from the coals, but dipped out the vegetables with a mountain-sheep horn spoon, into wooden bowls.

Sunflower meal of the parched seeds was also used to make sunflower seed balls; these were important articles of diet in olden times, and had a particular use.

For sunflower-seed balls I parched the seeds in a pot in the usual way, put them in a corn mortar and pounded them. When they were reduced to a fine meal, I reached into the mortar and took out a handful of the meal, squeezing it in the fingers and palm of my right hand. This squeezing it made it into a kind of lump or ball.

This ball I enclosed in the two palms and gently shook it. The shaking brought out the oil of the seeds, cementing the particles of the meal and making the lump firm. . . .

In olden times every warrior carried a bag of soft skin at his left side, supported by a thong over his right shoulder; in this bag he kept needles, sinews, awl, soft tanned skin for making patches for moccasins, gun caps, and the like. The warrior's powder horn hung on the outside of this bag.

In the bottom of this soft-skin bag the warrior commonly carried one of these sunflower-seed balls, wrapped in a piece of buffalo-heart skin. When worn with fatigue or overcome with sleep and weariness, the warrior took out his sunflower-seed ball, and nibbled at it to refresh himself. It was amazing what effect nibbling at the sunflower-seed ball had. If the warrior was weary, he began to feel fresh again; if sleepy, he grew wakeful.

Sometimes the warrior kept his sunflower-seed ball in his flint case that hung always at his belt over his right hip. It was quite a general custom in my tribe for a warrior or hunter to carry one of these sunflower-seed balls. We called the sunflower-seed ball mapi', the name for a sunflower. Sunflower meal, parched and pounded as described, was often mixed with corn balls, to which it gave an agreeable smell, as well as a pleasant taste.

From the foregoing accounts it should be clear that the sunflower was a useful plant to the Indians (whether or not it did all the things which it was reputed to do); but when the first Europeans reached this country, apparently sunflower cultivation was not widely practiced. Squash, beans, and maize were almost ubiquitous among agricultural Indians. Why was not the sunflower? It thrives under many climatic conditions, ranging from arid regions to those receiving moderately heavy rainfall. It is also most tolerant to differences in the length of growing season—it grows well not only in Mexico, where the plant requires seven months or more to mature seed, but also as far north as Canada, where it must complete its growing season in four months. The sunflower was certainly domesticated in temperate North America, and its cultivation here may well antedate that of maize. However, with the arrival of maize from Mexico the sunflower had to meet competition from one of the best food plants known to man. Maize makes an excellent meal, it stores as well as sunflowers, it grows as readily, and perhaps it was not as subject to as many insect and fungus diseases as have always plagued the sunflower. Moreover, no outer shell has to be

Achenes of a modern cultivated variety of sunflower (*above*) are compared with achenes from the Cramer Village archaeological site in Ohio. The archaeological material has been charred by fire and is probably 10 to 15 per cent smaller than it was originally.

Sunflower heads and fragments of heads from the Newt Kash Hollow Shelter archaeological site in Kentucky.

removed from the maize kernel in the preparation of meal. Probably the sunflower could not stand the competition—its spread was halted, and the plant was kept merely to add variety to the diet or for secondary uses—for oil or for dye. Many tribes, such as the Hidatsas, grew the plant only around the edge of the fields of corn.

Today a few Indian groups still grow their original strains of sunflower—the Hopis and the Havasupais in Arizona, the Mandans and Arikaras in North Dakota, and a few Iroquoian survivors in New York and Canada. These original Indian varieties are on the verge of extinction. Not only do they have considerable historical value but, equally important, they are quite different from our modern varieties of sunflower and hence might contain valuable germ plasm for in-

45

corporation into our varieties to develop superior plants. When it was realized a few years ago that the Indian varieties of maize were also rapidly disappearing, a group of interested scientists sponsored by the Rockefeller Foundation formed a "corn bank" to preserve this valuable germ plasm for future generations. "Seed banks" have now been established by various governments to preserve the primitive varieties of a number of crops, but it is already too late to save many of them, for they have disappeared as modern agriculture has spread. A few years ago I sent seeds of the Indian varieties of the sunflowers that I had grown to the United States Department of Agriculture, which plans to grow them every few years to keep the varieties available for plant breeders who might want to try them in sunflower-improvement programs.[2]

[2] Some scientists have recently suggested that certain areas where primitive agriculture is still practiced be set aside as "preserves" so that the crops now grown will continue to be cultivated. In putting forth this idea, noble as it may be to preserve germ plasm, they overlook one important fact. The people growing ancient varieties are often suffering from want of food and would gladly give up their old varieties for modern, higher-yielding strains. It is hardly fair to ask these people to continue to suffer from hunger to preserve their varieties for some possible future value to mankind.

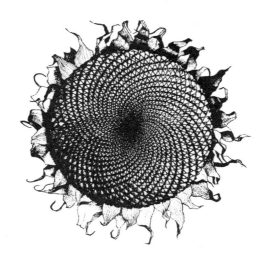

V

The Sunflower Reaches Europe
and Returns to America

THE FIRST European to see the sunflower in America will
probably forever remain nameless, but the credit for its introduction into Europe almost certainly belongs to the Spaniards. Although the early explorers of America were primarily
interested in gold, the wealth of plant life in the new world
did not escape their notice, and in the sixteenth century many
new plants were introduced into Europe. Potatoes, tomatoes,
peppers, maize, and many other American plants were introduced soon after the discovery of the Americas. Columbus
took back some of these plants from his travels, and other
plants shortly followed from Peru and Mexico and later from
other parts of the Americas.

The first published record of the sunflower appeared in
1568, written by the Belgian Rembert Dodoens, one of the

CHRYSANTH. PERVNIANVM.

many famous herbalists of the era. The herbalists wrote long books dealing with all the plants known to them. Their works provide a wealth of information for the modern student of plants; they enable one not only to date the introduction of many plants into Europe but also often to identify precisely the variety introduced. The fact that the sunflower was not known to the herbalists before the discovery of America is additional evidence, if it were needed, that the sunflower was American in origin.

After its introduction the sunflower was first grown as a curiosity, and by 1616 it was common in England. The herbalists were impressed by the plant with "stalkes . . . of the bignesse of a strong mans arme," which was said to grow to twenty-four feet in Spain, although fourteen feet was the best they could do in England.

One of the chief interests of the herbalists was the medicinal value of plants, and the early herbalists must have been sad indeed to report that "no virtues had yet been found" for the plant. Like the tomato and many other plants it had to wait some time before it became appreciated. In 1629, John Parkinson reported, "Sometimes the heads of the Sunne-Flower are dressed, and eaten as Hartichokes are, and are accounted of some to be good meate, but they are too strong for my taste." Others, however, found the buds very good, and the use of the flower head as a "dainty" persisted for some years. It is rather surprising that the use of the seeds for food was not discovered at that time; exactly when this discovery, or, rather, rediscovery, was made is not known. In 1699, John Evelyn wrote that he once made macaroons with the ripe, blanched seeds, "but the *Turpentine* did so domineer over all, that it did not answer expectation." Although it is true that the heads have a definite turpentine flavor, the seeds do not. Charles Bryant in 1783 stated that "the seeds have as agreeable flavor as Almonds and are excellent food for do-

The first illustration of the sunflower in Europe, from the herbal of Dodoens, 1568. Note the early name for the sunflower, *Chrysanthemum peruvianum.*

mestic poultry." Bryant also referred to the fact that "the seeds of this plant are copiously stored with oil, which may be easily expressed, and is not inferior to that drawn from Olives."[1]

In the previous chapter it was explained that the sunflower was native to North America, but Peru was at first regarded as the original home of the sunflower, a statement originating with Dodoens and echoed by many of the later herbalists. In fact, no less an authority than Alexander von Humboldt as late as the nineteenth century stated that "the *chimalatl*, or sun with the large flowers came from Peru to New Spain," and even today, in modern works dealing with cultivated plants, Peru is sometimes given as the place of origin of the sunflower. That the sunflower went to Europe from Peru seems most unlikely. There is no evidence that the sunflower was cultivated in any part of South America until recent times. It has not been recovered from archaeological sites there, it is not found as a decoration on pottery, nor was it reported by any of the early explorers in South America. Although it is grown there today, its cultivation is carried on primarily among the non-Indians of Argentina and other countries. Certain species of *Helianthus* grow naturally in Ecuador and Peru, but they are only distantly related to the cultivated sunflower and certainly could not have been the progenitor of the cultivated form.

It is curious that a mistake like this could be carried on, but it is not unique by any means, as we shall see when we examine the history of the Jerusalem artichoke in a later chapter. Peru was frequently the last port of call for the Spaniards before leaving for Europe, and it also was furnishing many new plants to Europe. Moreover, the name Peru may have been used by some writers of the time to refer to all of Span-

---

[1] I am indebted to Miss Alice M. Coats of England for certain of these references.

Groß Indianisch Flos Solis Peruuianus.
Sonnenblum.

Drawing of the sunflower from a later herbal (Mattiolus, 1586).

ish America, including Mexico, and not to the country in the restricted sense that we use it today.

From the descriptions in the herbals it seems likely that the sunflower was introduced from many different areas of North America, for in the early years after its introduction we find mentions of varieties with black, striped, and white seeds. It probably went to Spain from Mexico and from there rapidly spread to other parts of Europe, but there were almost certainly other introductions from America, with the likelihood that the English and French imported it from Virginia and Canada. It spread rapidly throughout Europe, but without spectacular success until it reached Russia. The story of its adoption there helps to explain why Russia soon became the foremost producer of sunflowers—a position it holds to this day.

The Holy Orthodox Church of Russia in the early nineteenth century observed very strict regulations governing the diet of the people during the forty days of Lent and the forty days preceding Christmas. A number of foods, including nearly all foods rich in oil, were prohibited during these periods, but the sunflower, which had only recently entered the country, was not on the list. The people eagerly adopted it, for it was a source of oil and could be eaten without breaking the letter of the law. As a result of this the popularity of the sunflower became immense.

Many people still think that the sunflower originated in Russia, largely perhaps because one of the best known varieties is the Mammoth Russian, or Russian Giant. The first colonists in the United States apparently did not grow the sunflower; if they did, it did not persist as a crop plant. It was not until the 1880's that the Mammoth Russian sunflower began to be offered by seed companies in this country. In 1893, Russian varieties were sent to this country from the

The drawings of the sunflower improved with time; this is from Renealmus, 1611. The previous two drawings were reproduced from woodcuts; this is apparently the first copperplate etching.

United States consul in St. Petersburg, and there was considerable enthusiasm about its development as a crop in the United States, but it did not catch on.

And so it was that the sunflower went to Europe from America, eventually reached Russia, and then was reintroduced into the Americas from Russia. Practically all the sunflowers now cultivated in the Americas are therefore of Russian origin. Little wonder that many people are inclined to think that the cultivated sunflower originated in Russia.

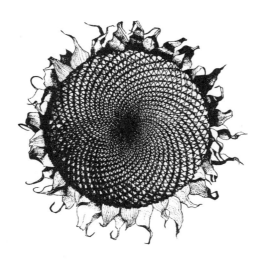

VI

The Sunflower Becomes a World Oil Crop

FROM A relatively minor crop for many years the sunflower
has gradually developed into one of the world's most important suppliers of vegetable oils. In the 1930's the sunflower
ranked tenth among the world's sources of vegetable oils. By
1950 it had risen to fourth place, behind the soybean, the peanut, and the cottonseed, and in 1970 it ranked second only to
the soybean. Its rise to prominence is not quite as spectacular
as that of the soybean, and the history of the two plants is
quite different. The soybean was introduced from the Far
East into the United States in 1804, but it was not until the
1930's that it made much of an impact on the economy of the
United States. Within a few years it became a major crop,
and the United States became the world's foremost producer.
The sunflower was introduced into Russia by way of Eastern

Harvesting sunflowers in the U.S.S.R. with a modern combine. Courtesy of N. Dvoryadkin.

Europe (the exact date unknown) and more gradually became a significant crop there. Whereas the soybean continues to be an important crop plant in its homeland, China, the sunflower has thus far amounted to little in its place of origin.

The modern history of the sunflower therefore is largely a Russian one. Today more than two-thirds of the world's cultivated sunflowers are grown in the Soviet Union, and they supply over 90 per cent of the vegetable oil in that country. The account of how the sunflower gained early acceptance was given in the previous chapter, but equally important to the success of the sunflower in the Soviet Union was that it was found to be a plant well adapted to many areas of the country. Presently some twelve million acres in Russia are devoted to the cultivation of sunflowers, principally in the Ukraine, northern Moldavia, the Volga area, and the central black-soil region.

According to some accounts that I have seen, one might conclude that at one time nearly all Russians went around with their pockets stuffed with sunflower achenes, munching on them all day long. It has been reported that in the days of the czars the soldiers received regular rations of sunflower seeds. There is no doubt that the eating of sunflower seeds is still extremely popular in the Soviet Union, more so than the peanut ever has been in the United States. Bowls of sunflower achenes have long been set out at parties and other social gatherings in the Soviet Union and the Balkan countries. One account volunteered by a Russian immigrant (slightly exaggerated perhaps) is that the Russian people can keep a continuous supply of achenes going into one side of the mouth and at the same time eject a continuous stream of hulls from the other side.

In addition to a great liking for sunflowers and having vast areas available for their cultivation, still another factor has been of great significance in making the Soviet Union the sunflower capital of the world. Shortly after the turn of the century the Russians devoted great effort to the improvement of the sunflower and to new ways of harvesting it. Interspecific hybridization was attempted as early as 1915 in an effort to secure disease resistance in the cultivated plant. Perhaps the most noteworthy achievement has been an increase in the oil content of the seed. Starting with varieties having an oil content of around 28 per cent in the 1920's, the Russian breeders increased this to 43 per cent by 1935 and to 49 per cent in 1955, and presently some varieties are reported with over 50 per cent oil content. Experiment stations were set up devoted primarily to the sunflower. Today the major sunflower research program is carried out at the All-Union Research Institute at Krasnodar. It would probably not be in error to state that more plant breeding with the sunflower has been carried out in the Soviet Union than in all the rest of the world's nations combined.

That the Russian sunflowers can play a very significant role in the world economy became evident in the late 1960's, when the Soviet Union began doubling its export of sunflower-seed

Drying sunflower heads in Dahomey. The method used for drying some of the traditional crops has been adopted for sunflowers. Courtesy of FAO, Rome, Italy.

oil. There was a record export of 787,000 tons in one year. The result was a drop in prices of all vegetable oils, much to the concern of the soybean growers in the United States. The soybean price dropped from eleven cents to seven cents a pound. Then as suddenly as the Soviet Union had dumped sunflower oil on the world market, it ceased to do so. The reason for the sudden export of huge quantities of sunflower oil by the Soviet Union remains unknown. Some have maintained that there was a surplus of sunflower oil in those years, but others have thought that they were actually depriving their own people of much-needed vegetable oil because of a need for hard money for purposes not yet entirely clear.

Although the sunflower is cultivated in many, if not most, other countries of the world, only a few have extensive areas devoted to it. Considerable acreage is grown in the Balkans and neighboring areas, particularly Romania, Bulgaria, Yugoslavia, Hungary, and Turkey. The crop has been of significance in some parts of Africa, Rhodesia being one of the leading producers. In the Americas sunflowers are important in Argentina, which for some time has ranked second only to Russia, with nearly three million acres devoted to sunflower cultivation. Sunflowers as a crop in Argentina date from 1870, and production was greatly stimulated during the Spanish Civil War, when supplies of olive oil from Spain were cut off.

During World War II vegetable oils became one of the products for which there was a great demand. In many countries this demand resulted in a new interest or a revival of interest in sunflowers. The Germans had other ideas about how to secure sunflower oil, however. In 1942, Hermann Göring told the German people that they would soon have more cooking oil from the conquered Russian sunflower fields.

Throughout the war years considerable work was done in England in an attempt to develop varieties suitable for that

A young lady examines a sunflower in Lebanon. The Food and Agricultural Organization has encouraged the growing of sunflowers to replace the Indian hemp or marijuana plant, now officially banned in Lebanon. Courtesy of FAO.

country. Seeds imported from Russia were renamed by the plant breeders so that the Germans would not know that Russian varieties could be grown in northern areas. Another reason for the name change was the feeling that the English farmers would have difficulty with the Russian names. Thus the Russian variety Cherniaka was changed to Jupiter, and Fuksinka became Mars. After the war interest in the sunflower waned in England, but the plant was on its way to becoming an important minor oil crop in Canada, particularly in Manitoba. The number of acres planted to sunflowers in that province increased from four thousand in 1943 to sixty thousand by 1949. In spite of the many difficulties that the Canadians had in the first few years—not least among which were various diseases of the plant, particularly rust—they have made the sunflower an economically successful crop. The efforts of the Canadian plant breeders to secure disease resistance and higher yields, and the improvements in planting and harvesting, have paid dividends, although the sunflower does not appear on its way to becoming a major crop. Only seventy-seven thousand acres were devoted to it in 1970.

Although there have been reports of the sunflower as an important "new" crop for the United States for over half a century, sunflowers have never lived up to expectations. Thus far the sunflower has been a minor crop plant in the United States, grown chiefly for bird feed and nutmeats for human consumption. In recent years, however, there have been attempts to promote the sunflower as an oil crop, and it may yet come into its own in its homeland.

It may seem strange to some that the sunflower has never amounted to much as a crop plant in its place of birth. But such a turn of events is not at all unusual among cultivated species. Coffee, native to Ethiopia, is cultivated much more extensively in the Americas today than it is in Africa. Just the reverse situation is found in cacao, the chocolate-bean plant, for it is native to the Americas, and today most of the world's cacao is grown in Africa. Many other such examples could be given. The usual explanation for this phenomenon is that a plant has acquired many enemies—both insect and

A field of cultivated sunflowers in Minnesota. Hives of honeybees are often placed near the fields to insure good pollination. Courtesy of Cargill.

fungal—in the area where it has been grown the longest, and when man introduces it into a new area, few, if any, of its natural enemies go with it.

This holds true to some extent for the sunflower, but it is certainly not the sole explanation for the failure of the sunflower to become well established as a cultivated plant in the United States. In the early days of agriculture no serious attempt was made to grow sunflowers as a crop plant in the American colonies. The effort was concentrated on the native maize, wheat, and many other Old World crops. As these crops were improved, it became more and more difficult for other plants to find a place on the farm. It should be noted, however, that both the peanut and the soybean were late entries on the agricultural scene in the United States, and both became quite successful. Edible oils are now supplied in some

Harvesting sunflowers in Minnesota. Courtesy of Cargill.

abundance by maize, soybeans, peanuts, and cottonseed, and it is difficult for the sunflower to compete with these well-established plants.

One of the early uses of the sunflower in the United States was for fodder and ensilage. Tests have shown that sunflower leaves and stems make good food for livestock, and the gigantic size of some of the older varieties and their rapid growth made them high yielders. They are still so used in a few areas, particularly where the growing season is too short for corn. Another early use, and still a fairly popular one, was as food for poultry.

The two major uses for sunflowers in the United States in recent years, however, have been as seeds for birds and as snacks in the human diet. Feeding wild birds has become increasingly popular, and probably most sunflowers grown in the United States are used for this purpose.

The habit of eating sunflower seeds is said to have been introduced by German and Russian immigrants, particularly the Mennonites, and for some time the achenes were called Russian peanuts in some areas. One variety of sunflower is known as Mennonite. The unshelled seeds never became a rival of the peanut in the United States, perhaps because the people never became proficient at shelling them in the mouth or because they considered this too indelicate a method of eating where company manners were required. In recent years shelled sunflower seeds have become available and appear to be growing in popularity.

At one time the chief producers among the states were California, Illinois, and Missouri. California still grows considerable acreage, but Illinois and Missouri are no longer important growers, having relinquished the lead to North Dakota and Minnesota. Sunflowers were found to be well adapted to the Red River Valley area of Minnesota, and the growth of sunflowers for oil production was started there in 1947 on an experimental basis. By 1967 growth was on a commercial basis. In 1968 fifty thousand acres were planted to sunflowers in that region for oil production, and about twice that amount was grown for the bird-seed trade. Different varieties are employed for the different purposes: the larger seeded types, including the old favorite, Mammoth Russian, in which oil content is not particularly important, are grown for human beings and birds. Smaller-seeded types, which have a high oil content, are used for oil production. Of the latter the two principal varieties in use at present are Armaneric and Krasnodnets. As the names indicate, both originated in the Soviet Union.

The sunflower oil produced in the United States is hardly competitive on the world market at present, but the interest and effort now being devoted to the plant indicate that it may yet become a significant crop in the United States. The more productive hybrid sunflowers that are beginning to appear (to be discussed in another chapter) could put the sunflower on a truly competitive basis with the other oil crops in this country. Moreover, it has been found that the sunflower is well adapted to the cotton-belt region, which would open vast new areas for sunflowers. Diseases are still a major problem, but after years of little breeding work on the sunflower in the United States, there is presently more effort being made along these lines. The sunflower will certainly continue to be grown for bird seed and human consumption and may yet make it as an oil crop in the United States.

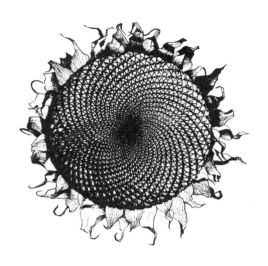

VII

The Uses of the Sunflower

ALTHOUGH nearly every part of the sunflower has been used by man in one way or another, it is the oil that is most valuable. Oils are high in energy and hence extremely important food sources for man. In recent years a great increase in the demand for oils of vegetable origin has resulted from their use in making margarine, which has largely replaced butter in many parts of the world. One important reason for the substitution of vegetable oils for animal oils for many purposes is that they are usually cheaper. Another reason of increasing importance in recent years is that most vegetable oils are polyunsaturated. Animal oils, on the other hand, are saturated and as such are suspected of being associated with heart disease in man. Naturally this has led to a greater use of plant oils in products where they can be substituted for animal oils. In addition to their use in food, some vegetable oils also find a number of uses in industry, as, for example, in the manufacture of soaps, paints, and linoleum.

Many species of plants are grown for their oils. Soybeans, corn, peanuts, coconuts, cotton, olives, oil palm, and flax are among some of the important ones. Their oils are sometimes classed as drying, semidrying, and nondrying. The sunflower is considered a semidrying oil and thus finds use in industry as well as for food. The sunflower's greatest competition comes from the soybean. Sunflower oil, however, is better nutritionally and more stable than soybean oil and hence is better for human use. At the same time it is better for use in making paints because it has a lower content of linolenic acid than does the soybean. Sunflower oil has long been used as a salad oil, considered equal to olive oil for that purpose by some people. It is also used in cooking and frying and for the manufacture of shortening and margarine. The high quality of the oil is, of course, one of the reasons for the rapid increase in the importance of the sunflower. Someday perhaps the sunflower may surpass the soybean in importance as far as oil is concerned. It will never replace the soybean, however, for its protein content does not reach the high levels found in the soybean.

The yield of vegetable oils has increased greatly in the developed nations of the world in recent years but has not shown the same dramatic growth in the developing countries. Yet it is the developing countries of the tropics which are experiencing the greatest growths in population and in which hunger is the most pronounced. Since these nations are too poor to import oils from the developed nations, they need more sources of their own. Thus far the soybean has been of limited success in tropical countries, and some people are looking to the sunflower as a potential oil resource in these areas. The sunflower, like the soybean, is not a tropical crop and whether it can fill the need remains to be seen.

The seed cake left after the oil is expressed from the seeds is a rich source of protein and is usually employed in sunflower-growing countries for feeding livestock. The sunflower

Agronomists examine sunflowers in a varietal trial in the Dominican Republic. In recent years the sunflower is being tried in a number of tropical and subtropical countries. Courtesy of FAO.

protein is of high quality but low in the amino acid lysine. Hence it is more highly recommended for animals of the ruminant group, such as cattle, sheep, and goats, than for the monogastric animals, such as chickens and hogs. In a hungry world in which protein is in great demand, the press cake from the oil crops is extremely important. Even if the protein of the seed cake is not used directly as a food source for man, its greater use in livestock feeding should make more of the cereals now used to feed animals available for human consumption.

71

Weed sunflowers as they appear in early winter. The sunflower is hardly attractive after it ceases blooming. The stems, however, have served for fuel.

A "flour" for humans was being made from sunflower seeds by the American Indians when the Europeans arrived. Although the flour is a good source of vitamins and minerals, as well as protein, it is not now generally used. A quarter of a century ago the Vio-Bin Corporation of Illinois tried to market a sunflower flour, but the attempt was unsuccessful because the company could not secure an adequate supply of seeds from the local farmers, who found it more profitable to grow soybeans. The flour could not be used alone for baking because of the high oil content, but mixed with wheat flour it was found to make cakes and other bakery goods as good as, or better than, those made from wheat flour alone.

The seed hulls, or shells (the fruit or achene coat), ordinarily removed before oil extraction were for a long time discarded, used for "litter" for poultry, or returned to the soil. A few years ago it was found that the hulls could be used for fuels, and for several years Co-op Vegetable Oils, Limited, of Canada pressed the hulls into logs, which were found to be superior to coal for some purposes and also could be used in fireplaces and in cookstoves. Other uses of the hulls were discovered in the Soviet Union; today they are used in that country in manufacturing ethyl alcohol and furfural, in lining plywood, and in growing yeast.

The dried stems of sunflowers have also been used for fuel, particularly in the Soviet Union. An unusual story connected with such a use comes from the United States. According to a teacher in a one-room school in Kansas, in times past it was the custom for the first youngster to arrive to start the fire for the day. One cold day a pupil burned all of the coal in short order, and the students had to gather stalks from wild sunflowers to keep the fire going. The teacher reported that it took a lot of sunflowers to keep them warm. Indeed, it must have, for dried sunflower stems burn very rapidly. I have found them to make excellent kindling to start a fire.

It is probably wasteful to use sunflower stems for fuel, unless the ashes are returned to the soil. Sunflowers, particularly the old-fashioned giant varieties, are rank feeders, and for this reason the stems should be incorporated back into the soil to replace in part what they have taken from it.[1] The stems contain fairly high amounts of phosphorous and potassium and are sometimes composted to be returned to the soil as fertilizer.

The stems have also been used as a source of commercial fiber. The Chinese reportedly have used this fiber for the manufacture of fabrics. Experiments with its use for paper

---

[1] If one plans to grow sunflowers in the same place year after year, it is best to use the stems for fertilizer in some other area, for the practice of returning them to the soil that is to grow sunflowers again may serve to perpetuate certain sunflower diseases.

Although bees are the most common visitors to sunflowers, many other insects, such as this Monarch butterfly, also find them attractive.

production have been carried out in a number of countries, and it shows some promise for this purpose. In the Soviet Union the stalks have been made into a light-weight acoustical-ceiling tile. The pith of the stems was once used to make life preservers in Russia. According to one report, the sunflower pith has a greater buoyancy than either cork or reindeer's hair. The dried leaves have been used as a substitute for tobacco, and the roasted seeds have been used as a coffee substitute. Neither report, however, indicated how it tasted in these roles.

The use of the seeds for human food, probably the most ancient use, and for wild and domesticated birds has been sufficiently mentioned in previous chapters and needs little elaboration here except to point out that in recent years the seeds have been eagerly adopted by health-food fanciers. Some people grow a few sunflowers to attract birds to their garden. Many persons also grow the giant sunflowers simply because they feel that they are an ornament for the garden. Other varieties of the common sunflower, as well as other species of the genus, are more commonly grown as ornamentals, however, and they will form the subject of a later chapter. Many seed companies offer seeds of the giant varieties for those who may want to try them. Not long ago I saw a cartoon in a magazine in which one garden-club lady is saying to another, "When the other flowers in my garden see the sunflower they give up." There perhaps is a grain of truth in this, for few garden flowers grown close to the sunflower can compete for nutrients and light. In addition to its ornamental value the sunflower is attractive to bees and makes a good honey plant.

Frequently overlooked in the uses of some plants is their important role in teaching and in pure research. Probably no other plants—unless it is the cocklebur—has been used more in plant physiology than the sunflower. The ease with which the sunflower can be grown and its rapid growth make it a favorite experimental plant. Few courses in botany are complete without a study of its seed structure. Countless biology students have looked at slides of cross sections of the sunflower stem in an attempt to understand the internal structure of plants. The flower head, because of its large size, serves as an excellent example of the structure of the composite type of flower.

Just as had the Indians, the Europeans found medicinal uses for the sunflower. Whether such use was acquired directly from the Indians or discovered independently is not entirely clear, but there is some reason for believing the latter, since the early herbalists did not report any medicinal virtues. The greatest medicinal use for the sunflower throughout the world has been for pulmonary affections. That is of some interest because it will be recalled that this was the plant's chief medicinal use among the Indians. A preparation of the seeds has been widely used for colds and coughs, and was said to be particularly valuable for the relief of whooping cough. In the Caucasus the seeds have served as a substitute for quinine in the treatment of malaria, reportedly with favorable results. Although the sunflower has no official standing in medicine today, it is still listed in modern herb manuals. A recipe for a preparation that has been found "efficacious" given in one modern herbal calls for more gin than sunflower seeds. Perhaps even if it does not cure, it leaves the user happy. As for the real medicinal value of sunflowers, the words of Laurence Johnson in his *Medical Botany* of 1884 are worth quoting: "Sunflower seeds are said to be diuretic and expectorant but there is little reason for believing them medicinal."[2]

Sunflower pith has been used by the Portuguese in making *moxa*, which was used in the cauterization of wounds and infections. *Moxa* was placed on the area to be treated and ignited. The burn might be severe enough to result in scars, but it supposedly healed. Except in cases of severe infection this treatment was hardly to be recommended, for the burn could be worse than the original infection. Other medicines were found to do the job more effectively and without leaving scars.

An infusion from the flowers has been used to kill flies. Tests have shown that aqueous extracts of the flowers are toxic to mice but not to rabbits.

Even though the Russians are the greatest users of sunflowers today, probably no man has been more enthusiastic about the sunflower than an American, J. I. Rodale, who until his death in 1971 was editor of the magazine *Organic Gardening*. In a little booklet entitled *Sunflower Seed, the Miracle Food*, he described with considerable rapture his and others' experiences with the sunflower, finding values in the sunflower that the Indians never dreamed of. In the space of

[2] But perhaps the sunflower should not yet be written off as a medicinal plant, for just as I was ready to send this manuscript off to press a friend of mine brought in a newspaper article reporting that a group of British doctors had discovered that sunflower oil may help in the treatment of multiple sclerosis. The doctors claim that people suffering from this disease lack linoleic acid, which the sunflower oil supplies in some abundance.

A goldfinch feeds on a sunflower. Courtesy of Lewis Johnson.

three pages he stated that eating sunflower seeds reduces cavities in the teeth, stops pink toothbrush, aids quivering eyes, improves the eyes so that they are not troubled by snow blindness, and meliorates the condition of the skin. Elsewhere in this pamphlet we learn from testimonials that the sunflower removes the unpleasant coating on the tongue, is good for the nerves, relieves soreness in the muscles, and eliminates that tired feeling. One is inclined to suggest perhaps that sunflower seeds should be taken with a grain of salt. There is no doubt that sunflower seeds are a fine food, but after all there must be limits.

One is tempted to go on discussing Rodale's remarkable little booklet. For example, the sunflower is "drenched with sun-vitality" because the head follows the sun, ending up facing the west "to absorb the few last rays of the dying sun."

This he suggested as a possible reason why the sunflower is immune to diseases that affect other plants. (According to most studies the sunflower is host to as many, if not more, diseases than most of our commonly cultivated plants.) Rodale also credited Columbus with noting the popularity of the sunflowers among the Indians and being instrumental in its introduction into Europe. There is no record that the sunflower was cultivated in the lands that Columbus visited; if he ever saw a sunflower, he failed to mention it. As for his being instrumental in its introduction into the Old World, are we to assume that if Columbus had not discovered America the sunflower would never have reached Europe?

Now that we have learned something of the history and uses of the sunflower, it is time to give some consideration to how the Indians made a cultivated plant out of a wild one. Thus far the discussion has been mainly factual; the next chapter will involve considerable speculation.

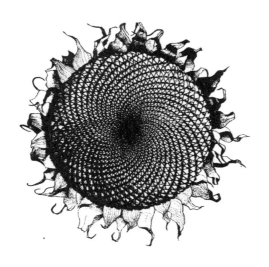

VIII

A Weed Becomes Respectable

THE ORIGIN of a cultivated plant is a gradual process, not a single event, and it is obvious that for this and other reasons it is difficult to state exactly where and when the sunflower became domesticated. At best only a general area where the domestication probably occurred and an approximate date can be designated. The sunflower is not alone in this respect, for the early history of our ancient cultivated plants is only vaguely known, and mysteries still surround the origins of many of our food plants. The study of their origins cannot be attacked experimentally in the usual sense of the word—or only rarely so—but scattered facts can be brought to bear on the subject so that reasonable hypotheses can be erected to replace pure speculation.

Agriculture apparently had several independent origins

around the world. The earliest evidence is from the Near East, around nine thousand years ago. Most of our food plants, including the two most important, wheat and rice, come from the Old World. Two or three thousand or so years later agriculture began in the New World. The archaeological evidence indicates that it was in Mexico and Peru that farming was first practiced in the New World. Mexico has given us corn, some squashes, the common bean, peppers, and several other plants. Such important food plants as the Irish potato, peanuts, the tapioca plant, and tomatoes are among those that we know had their origins in South America. These efficient food plants allowed the development of the civilizations of the Aztecs, Mayas, and Incas, but we know that the food plants were in cultivation long before those high cultures appeared on the scene.

The sunflower is unique among the early American cultivated food plants, for it is the only one to have been domesticated in what was to become the United States. Moreover, the wild plant that gave rise to the cultivated one has been identified with some certainty. As a cultivated plant, however, the sunflower appears to be much more recent than plants with their origins in Latin America.

Our story begins once more with the use of wild sunflowers by certain Indians. Wild sunflowers must have been common in western North America, and many groups of Indians must have gathered the seeds for thousands of years in the prehistoric period. Where these wild sunflowers came from is not entirely clear, and to go into that story would unduly complicate matters. It is fairly certain, however, that sunflowers were evolving long before man made his appearance. Although today the common sunflower of the western United States is mostly a plant of roadsides and waste areas, it must have been growing in a truly wild state when man first began to use the seeds.

As man began to use the plant, seeds were carried from place to place. Seeds scattered accidentally might find the new habitats around the Indian villages suitable for their growth. Thus the plant may have become a camp-following

The size of the sunflower head increases with domestication: wild sunflower (*lower left*), weed sunflower (*upper left*), domesticated sunflower (*right*).

weed, and was spread to new areas as the Indians moved. Although the plant was not yet a specific object of cultivation, the first close link to man had been made. We do not know the exact area or how large an area the common wild sunflower occupied before man came, but it certainly seems that the plant was spread by man into many new areas from its original home in the Southwest—west to California, south to Texas, and east across the Mississippi River. For hundreds or thousands of years the plant probably changed only slightly, but gradually there began to evolve a special weed in the eastern area of its range. The most significant feature about this new plant was that it could grow only in the disturbed

81

sites around Indian villages, and it also had larger heads and consequently larger achenes, which meant that it was an even better food plant than the original wild type. Today this eastern weedy form of the common sunflower is recognized as distinct from that of the western United States, although the two intergrade over a broad area. In the eastern area, when the weed sunflower came into being, it did not meet the competition from its relative in the west, and it was possible for the larger-headed form to maintain itself, since it could not be hybridized out of existence by the western form. Man probably had little to do with the evolution of this new weed other than to carry it from place to place—the larger seeds probably enabled the plant to survive better as a weed. The next stage in the development of the plant, however, required the active participation of man.

The next change, a gene mutation, was a relatively simple one that occurred spontaneously. It caused the plant to fail to produce branches, so that a single large head was produced instead of the many small heads characteristic of the wild and weed sunflowers. This change may have occurred in wild populations of the sunflower, or the Indians may have already started to cultivate the branched weed sunflower and the mutation arose in the cultivated plants. The change could have occurred more than once, but, in any event, somewhere a man had the vision to save seeds of the new plant instead of eating them all. The new plant that arose as a result of this mutation was hardly the same as the one that European man found the Indians cultivating. Other mutations occurred, some of which may have led to further increase in seed size. Again, if seeds were saved from these plants, a sunflower with larger seeds could evolve, so that in time the Indians had a sunflower that produced achenes three times the size of those of the wild plants.

The development of a cultivated plant may seem relatively simple to us, for the cultivation of plants appears so obvious. But this simple act of cultivation was instrumental in the development of civilization. Alphonse de Candolle, the world's foremost student of cultivated plants in the nineteenth cen-

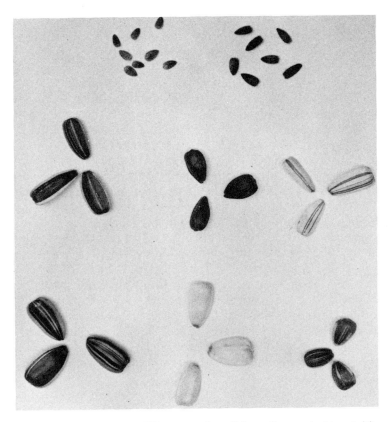

Achenes of sunflowers (*H. annuus*): wild sunflower (*upper left*); weed sunflower (*upper right*); modern domesticated varieties (*bottom two rows*).

tury, wrote: "In the progress of civilization the beginnings are usually feeble, obscure, and limited. There are reasons why this should be the case with the first attempt at agriculture or horticulture."

But why should plants be cultivated when wild plants can be used? At one time it was popular to think that people became agriculturists because of the need for food, but the idea that necessity is the mother of invention has largely been discarded in modern theses on the origin of agriculture. People who have to spend most of their time getting enough food to eat do not have the time to domesticate plants. Cultivation requires a great interest in individual plants and also leisure for "experimenting." While cultivated plants do not require constant attention, one can hardly expect simply to plant seeds and come back a few months later to harvest the crop.

We do not know what first stimulated the human animal to plant seeds. Perhaps, as is true with many inventions, accident was involved to some extent. Seeds that were dropped near the village site were observed to grow into plants the next year, and it was realized that seeds gave rise to more plants like the ones from which they came. Such an observation must have happened more than once among primitive seed collectors, but the next step, the intentional planting of seeds, took some initiative. Perhaps religion was involved in the origin of planting. Primitive man, we know, believed that spirits existed in plants. In order to make the plants or their seeds safe to eat and to assure a bountiful harvest in the following season, he often returned some seeds to the spirits. Such ceremonies still come down to us in "first-fruit" and "last-sheaf" celebrations of the harvest. Could the returning of the first fruits to the mother earth somehow have led eventually to the intentional planting of seeds?

Perhaps we shall never know exactly what led man to plant seeds, but it seems certain that the idea of planting occurred more than once, for it is fairly obvious that the invention of agriculture developed independently in both the Old World and the New. In fact, it may have had several origins in both places. This raises an interesting question in regard to the sunflower. Was the sunflower first cultivated by Indians who had no previous conception of agriculture, or was the sunflower domesticated after the North American Indians had acquired the idea of agriculture from their southern neighbors? The belief commonly held today is that agriculture in temperate North America was not an original development but came from Mexico. One good reason for this assumption is that most of the plants cultivated north of Mexico are plants native to Central and South America and Mexico—beans, gourds, squash, and, most important of all, corn. The acquisition of these plants and presumably the knowledge of how to grow them traveled north through exchange or migrations from the south. No prehistoric cultures rivaling those of Mexico, Central America, and Peru were attained in temperate North America, a fact perhaps indicating that the cultivated plants necessary for a high culture had not been in temperate North America for long enough time.

We know from archaeologists' findings that the Indians of the Southwest—the Hopis and their precursors—were advanced farmers. Although they perhaps did not bring many new plants into cultivation, they developed many new varieties from old stocks. When these peoples were discovered by Europeans, they were growing sunflowers. Wild sunflowers are certainly abundant in the Southwest. Could it be that sunflowers were first domesticated in that area? This cannot be proved or disproved, but the fact that cultivated sunflowers have never been found in archaeological sites in the Southwest may be significant. Even more significant, however, is the fact that wild sunflowers were found along with other cultivated species in archaeological sites in New Mexico. It seems likely that the Indians of the Southwest acquired the cultivated sunflower from elsewhere and that its acquisition was fairly recent.

If we examine the locations where prehistoric cultivated sunflowers have been found, we see that they are concentrated in what may broadly be designated as the middle area of temperate North America (see map, page 37)—the area in which we find weed sunflowers growing today. It is in this general region that I am inclined to look for the first domestications —maybe one or maybe more points of origins—of the cultivated sunflower. The archaeological evidence we have is tantalizing. Although it is clear that Indians were growing sunflowers in no way inferior to modern varieties in size, we cannot be sure whether or not they had corn and other Mexican plants at the time they were domesticating the sunflower. Although most of the archaeological sunflower finds are associated with other members of the typical food complex of the North American Indians, a few specimens have been found that were not associated with other cultivated plants. However, it is not entirely clear whether these are of wild or of domesticated sunflowers.

In many places the archaeological record can be read like a book; the removal of layer after layer of soil reveals earlier cultures so that a definite sequence of events can be recorded. Unfortunately, this is not always the situation in the cave and cliff dwellings, where most of the remains of the sunflowers have been found. Moreover, the earliest investigations of these sites were not always systematic, and we cannot be sure which plants are early and which are late in a particular locality. Amateurs, arrowhead hunters, and others seeking curios to sell to tourists have frequently despoiled the record. Such people in their search for the more conspicuous remains of ancient cultures have thrown aside plant remains, little realizing or caring that they were destroying all chances that the scientist would ever be able to reconstruct the story of the peoples who lived there thousands of years ago.

No extremely early dates have been set on any of the sunflower seeds that have been recovered. However, a radiocarbon date for the Kentucky cliff dwellers who had sunflowers has been established as early as twenty-six hundred years ago. Corn was definitely in the Southwest at that time and was probably in the East by that date. On other lines of evidence it has been suggested that these cliff-dwelling Indians may have been in existence as long as ten thousand years ago, but it is unlikely that intentional cultivation would have been practiced at that early time.

In a recent excavation of Salts Cave, in Mammoth Cave National Park in Kentucky, under the direction of Betty Jo Watson, remains of sunflowers have been found going back to approximately 1500 B.C. Evidence of squash, a plant of Mexican origin, does not occur until much later, and no corn or beans were found. On this basis one anthropologist, Richard Yarnell, suggests that sunflower cultivation was being practiced in eastern North America before the arrival of cultivated plants from Mexico. Admittedly this is slender evidence, but once these people had the superior food plants that came from Mexico, why would they bother domesticating the sunflower? The question might also be asked, Why did they domesticate sunflowers but not other plants? Here again the evidence is puzzling, but it appears that at least one other plant was being cultivated.

From the material left behind in the Ozarks and Kentucky we know that the Indians hunted small game and collected nuts and seeds. Among the seeds are those of *Chenopodium album* (lamb's-quarters). Other species of this genus are known to have been cultivated—and still are cultivated—for food in Mexico and the Andes. Although some have maintained that these weeds were also cultivated in temperate North America, there is no evidence that would prove or disprove this theory. Achenes of two other plants, *Ambrosia* (ragweed) and *Iva* (marsh elder, or sumpweed), have also been found at some of the archaeological sites. These are both native to the region and, like the sunflower, are members of the composite family. The ragweed seeds recovered were thought at first to be larger than seeds of the ragweed that we know today, but this has recently been shown to be erroneous. There is no doubt, however, that the seeds of the marsh elder which the Indians had were much larger than those of the wild plant. It seems possible then that the large size of these seeds, like those of the sunflowers, resulted from cultivation and selection.

We, of course, do not know definitely that the Indians were using ragweed and marsh-elder seeds for food. They could have been used medicinally or ceremonially, but we are probably safe in assuming that the Indians used them for food the way they did other seeds. One botanist who puzzled over this problem went so far as to cook some ragweed seeds and commented that they were "palatable and rich in food values."

With the exception of the sunflower, none of these plants was found in cultivation in historic times. They disappeared among the Indians as mysteriously as they had appeared. Their prominence was brief. Could they have been the victims of the superior food plants which came up from Mexico, a fate that almost caught the sunflower? Only the sunflower lingered on to add variety to the diet and to supply oil and coloring matter.

Little is known about the peoples who were using the ragweed and marsh elder along with the sunflower. Their culture lasted until nearly 1750, according to the anthropologists, and, if Coronado had taken a route a little more to the north when he crossed the continent, we might have had historical records of these peoples. That they were still using ragweed and marsh elder at this late date is unlikely, for by this time they had corn.

When European man came across America, he found the sunflower cultivated in many different places. The plants he saw were by no means uniform—the Indians of different areas had developed the sunflower to suit their special needs. The Hopis had a purple-shelled form which could be used for dye as well as for food. Moreover, this sunflower was well adapted to the semiarid conditions of the Southwest, and the seeds could be planted several inches deep so that they could get enough moisture to germinate in that environment. The plant took five months or longer to produce mature seed, while at the same time the Indians of Canada had a plant that could mature in their short growing season of four months. Some groups had forms with dark achenes; others had striped or white achenes. In a sense the Indians were great plant breeders, but what they did with sunflowers is minor compared to what they accomplished with corn, varieties of which were produced to meet almost every need. When we realize that not one of our important food plants has been developed in historical time, we appreciate the great contributions of the early farmers and "plant breeders." No important new food plants have originated in historic times simply because our ancestors had already done such a tremendous job in this direction that it was unnecessary. We have for the most part simply improved the plants they handed down to us.

That is precisely what has happened with the sunflower. To summarize: Early man in America found that the seeds were a good food. The plant became a camp-following weed and was introduced into new areas. Gradually there evolved a special weedy race well adapted to disturbed sites around villages in the central area. Man deliberately began cultivating this weed, either before or after the occurrence of a mutation that produced an unbranched plant with a single head. Selection of other mutants by the Indian improved the plant and gave rise to a variety of types. The modern plant breeder has taken over this plant, increased the oil content, and bred dwarf forms that can be harvested with modern farm machinery. Thus the sunflower, like oats, rye, and some of our other food plants, is a weed that made good.

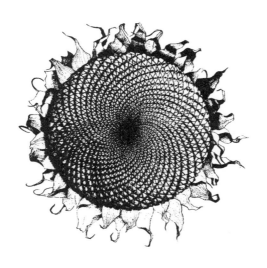

IX

More About Weeds

And the yellow sunflower by the brook in autumn
beauty stood.
    —William Cullen Bryant, "The Death of the Flowers"

MY STUDY of the sunflower has taken me to many interesting
places, from the Keys of Florida and the coastal range of
California to the Andes of Ecuador. But when sunflowers
come to mind, I always see first the dump heaps of St. Louis
and the railroad yards of East St. Louis, where they grow in
great profusion, for it was there that I made my acquaintance
with the sunflower. The sunflower by the brook is not our
common sunflower. The fact of the matter is that the common
sunflower most often is a weed.

Some would say a weed is a plant "out of place"; others,

These sunflowers are just coming into bloom on a vacant lot in East St. Louis, Illinois.

somewhat facetiously perhaps, would say that it is a plant whose virtues have not yet been discovered. Another might say that it is "any injurious, troublesome or unsightly plant that is at the same time useless or comparatively so." The sunflower may be injurious when it is a weed in a corn or soybean field, but it is causing little trouble on a dump heap in St. Louis, and in fact, it considerably improves the appearance of such places. Although it was this weed that gave birth to the cultivated sunflower, it is a weed for all of that.

What is a weed then? No one definition will serve, but among those who have studied weeds it is generally accepted that they are usually plants that grow in places that have been recently disturbed in some way, usually by man or the animals that live with him. Thus some plants, such as the beautiful California poppies, may at the same time be considered both weeds and wild flowers, depending on where they are growing. Weeds, then, are plants of pastures, cultivated fields, fence rows, roadsides, railroad tracks, vacant lots, and other waste places—all environments that are largely manmade. They are seldom found in virgin woods or unpastured mountain meadows. Weeds are sometimes said to be aggressive plants, but this is true only in that they invade bare areas or that they will grow in places where other plants will not thrive. They compete with cultivated plants but not with wild ones. In a sense weeds need man's care, for it has been shown that if a cultivated field is abandoned the annual weeds come in and are replaced by perennial weeds, and, as time goes on, if man does not redisturb the environment by plowing or other acts, the wild plants that grew in the region before man first turned the sod once more may take over.

Before man came on the scene, the precursors of weeds were plants that grew on naturally disturbed areas—flood plains of rivers, burned-over areas, and places disturbed by animals. Herds of buffaloes and other large animals could do considerable damage to the natural vegetation of an area. As Edgar Anderson has pointed out, the dinosaurs in a single meal could wreak havoc on the natural vegetation. These preweeds were ready to move in, once man came along and began to change the earth's surface in a way that it had never been changed before. As time went on, other wild plants became adapted to the newly disturbed environments so that in a short time a whole new weedy flora came into existence —many plants changing so radically that new species came into being. Some of the weeds, like the sunflower, became food plants for man and in time became the direct object of man's attention. In fact, many of the lowly weeds, such as rye and oats, became some of our most important cultivated plants.

Almost every plant family has contributed to our weedy flora—the composite family has been particularly prominent in this connection. Botanists of earlier generations tried to draw up a list of characteristics of weeds, and they found that weeds often produced large numbers of long-lived seeds and possessed efficient means of seed dispersal. Let us examine the sunflower to see whether any of these characteristics can explain its spread and success on newly disturbed areas.

The production of huge numbers of seeds is found in some of our most successful weeds. A single plant of hedge mustard (*Sisymbrium officinale*) may produce as many as 200,000 seeds, and the pigweeds (*Amaranthus*) can almost match this number. Frequently correlated with seed output is seed weight, with plants of open habitats generally having light, small seeds. However, the common sunflower will produce only at the most a few thousand seeds on a single plant, and moreover, the "seed" is fairly large as seeds go.

It has also been found that many weeds have extremely efficient methods of seed dispersal. The milkweed and the dandelion have a parachute device; others, such as the stick-tight and the wild carrot have special methods for dispersal by sticking to animals. As was pointed out in the first chapter, many of the sunflower's relatives have special adaptations for efficient seed dispersal, but the sunflower has none.

If we inquire how the sunflower gets around, we find that surprisingly little is known about the subject. We do know that the achenes of the sunflower are eagerly sought by birds and small mammals. With many plants the fruits or seeds are eaten whole, and seeds may pass through the digestive tract of the animal unharmed. In fact, with certain seeds this process may be necessary for successful germination—the action of the enzymes of the animal's digestive system may help to break down hard seed coats so that germination occurs. Moreover, when it is excreted by the animal, the seed is provided with a little fertilizer to help it get off to a good start in life. However, mice and birds crack the sunflower achene and eat only the kernel, which may be digested completely. Nevertheless, birds and small mammals probably play an important role in the dissemination of the achenes. They may be stored by mice and never eaten. Birds lighting on a mature sunflower head may shake some of the achenes to the ground. Obviously not all the seeds are eaten or the plant would be extinct. Rarely some achenes may remain in the head over winter and not reach the ground until the next spring after snow and rain have knocked the plant to the ground. Man also must be an important agent in the spread of the seeds, as well as providing the proper environment for their subsequent growth. The sunflower's wide distribution along roadsides and railroad right of ways is primarily dependent upon man. Grading and other road operations, movement of farm machinery, and the like are important in the spread of seeds.

Thus, although the sunflower is not provided with any special method of dissemination, it manages to get around very well. It is by no means unique in this regard, for many plants without obvious means of seed dissemination manage to attain as wide a distribution as those with special means of transport by wind, water, or animals.

Turning now to another possible factor in the success of some weeds, we find that there is great variation in how long seeds retain their capacity to germinate. Many weeds are able to maintain their viability for long periods of time. Our knowledge of this subject is due in large measure to a man who started an experiment the results of which are still being tabulated years after his death. In 1879, W. J. Beal, a professor of botany at Michigan Agricultural College (now Michigan State University), collected seeds of a number of plants and placed them in bottles, which were then buried in the soil. At intervals of five years up to 1920 and at intervals of ten years since that time seeds were removed from the bottles and their germination tested. After seventy years it was found that seeds of the evening primrose (*Oenothera biennis*), dock (*Rumex crispus*), and mullein (*Verbascum blattaria*)—all "good" weeds—still retained the power to germinate. A Danish botanist who made a study of seeds from archaeological sites found that certain weed seeds remained viable for one hundred to six hundred years and that seeds of two of them, lamb's-quarters and corn spurry (*Spergula arvensis*), had seeds that would still germinate after having been buried seventeen hundred years. Little wonder that the life of the farmer is a continual battle with weeds—he may still be fighting the offspring of weeds that his grandfather had allowed to become established. The characteristic of long-lived seeds may be shared by nonweeds. The record apparently belongs to an arctic lupine. Seeds of *Lupinus arcticus* are reported to have germinated after having been buried and frozen ten thousand years ago. Lupines belong to the bean family, members of which frequently have seeds with impervious seed coats that allow the seed a very long life. Reports of the germination of wheat seeds several thousand years old from Egyptian pyramids have never been verified scientifically. It seems likely that those seeds of "mummy" wheat that germinate are recent grains that have been previously planted by guides to be found by gullible tourists.

Unfortunately, Beal did not include the sunflower in his experiment. It seems likely that the sunflower possesses no great distinction in this regard, and, like seeds of most plants, the viability is lost rapidly after a few years. I have found that seeds air-dried and then stored at low temperatures gave 50 per cent germination after fifteen years. However, these are ideal storage conditions and are probably seldom or never met in nature.

While the production of many seeds, efficient methods of seed transport, and long-lived seeds may contribute to the success of some weeds, there are many nonweedy species that possess these traits and many weeds, including the common sunflower, that do not. Therefore, we must look to other factors to explain the success of the common sunflower as a weed.

To do so, it is first necessary to explain briefly why any plant grows where it does. Three basic factors control plant distribution, and these are obvious when one stops to think about the subject. First and foremost is climate—primarily temperature and rainfall; second is the type and nature of the soil; and third, working within the limits imposed by the first two, is the biotic factor, the interrelationships of a plant to other organisms, both plant and animal, including man (we have already seen man's importance in providing habitats for weeds). The interaction of these factors is often complex.

The common wild sunflower is found throughout much of North America[1] from southern Canada to northern Mexico, from sea level to altitudes of over seven thousand feet. It is found in the Southwest, where the rainfall is only a few inches a year, as well as in more mesophytic areas in the East. Since it is an annual, it can stand extreme winters, for it is only necessary that the seed survive. Thus, as long as there is plenty of sunlight—for the sunflower cannot tolerate dense shading—it will grow in a wide range of climates. It also shows considerable tolerance for varying soil types. It will grow in moderately heavy soils, clay loams, or rubbish heaps in which the chief component may be cinders, but it is seldom found in sandy soils. For the most part it grows only in well-drained soils, but one variety from southern California grows in the early part of the season in shallow pools of water which dry up as the season advances.

In much of its range the sunflower is common as a roadside plant or a weed in abandoned fields. In some areas, for example, in parts of Oklahoma and Kansas, it is often the first plant to invade a field the year after the farmer ceases to use it for crops. It is frequently the pioneer weed and often constitutes the dominant vegetation in such areas for the first two years. After two or three years, however, the sunflowers disappear rapidly and are replaced by a grass, *Aristida oligantha*. In 1968, Roger Wilson and Elroy Rice studied such fields and found that some of the other plant species growing near sunflowers showed reduced growth. Experiments revealed that sunflowers produce a toxic substance that inhibits the growth of a number of plants, including sunflowers themselves. Its lack of effect upon *Aristida oligantha*, however, enabled grass to replace the sunflowers in a few years.

The ability of some plants to give off a toxic substance that prevents or inhibits the growth of other species is one example

---

[1] But, unlike many weeds, it has never really made much of a mark for itself as a weed on other continents.

of a biotic factor, mentioned previously. The fact that sunflowers may give off a toxic substance provides some understanding of the success of the plant as a weed, but it is hardly a complete answer. For example, in some parts of its range the sunflower may come up year after year in the same field. Either the self-toxicity found in the laboratory with Oklahoma sunflowers may be lacking in plants in other areas, or it operates in nature quite differently from its behavior in the laboratory.

In the eastern half of the United States the sunflower is mostly confined to vacant lots and railroad yards of cities, such as in St. Louis and Indianapolis, where I know it best. In some places in these cities it grows in a soil—if, indeed, the substrate can be dignified by that name—in which there may be a considerable amount of cinders but also a sprinkling of beer cans, broken bottles, and other debris. It is not an attractive habitat and is one that even most weeds appear to shun. No detailed studies have been made about why sunflowers grow in such places, but I have puzzled over it.

Many years ago it occurred to me that perhaps such habitats provided some mineral element necessary for the good growth of sunflowers, but I decided that this was unlikely when I found that the plants, grown from seed, would also do very well in my garden outside the city. Another possibility suggested itself. Perhaps there was some toxic element present in these soils that sunflowers could tolerate but most other plants could not. Thus sunflowers could grow here largely free from competition with most other species. This hypothesis has yet to be tested.

On the other hand, perhaps the soil has little or nothing to do with the sunflower's seeming predilection for dump heaps in the larger cities. Dump heaps, as well as railway yards, are usually in greatest profusion in the industrial areas. Could it be that it is an ability to thrive in the polluted atmosphere of such areas that explains why sunflowers can grow there? It is known that many plants have a low tolerance to smoke, and thus the sunflowers might have little competition in such habitats.

The prairie sunflower (*H. petiolaris*), often a weed in sandy places.

While it appears that we still have much to learn about the ecology of the sunflower, I think it can be said that it owes its great success as a weed to the fact that it is both a plastic and a variable species. The same statement can be made about many other wide-ranging weeds. Such species can adapt themselves to a great variety of climatic, soil, and biotic factors and thereby attain wide distribution. In a later chapter some explanation will be provided for the sunflower's great variability.

So far the remarks on weedy helianthi have been confined to the common sunflower, but the genus has several other representatives that qualify as weeds. The prairie sunflower (*H. petiolaris*) frequently behaves like a weed in areas of sandy soil. Before 1900 this species was largely, if not entirely, restricted to the western United States but it is now spreading east of the Mississippi River. Some of the other annual sunflowers, such as *H. bolanderi* in California, have weedy tendencies, but none of them has attained the wide distributions of the common sunflower and *H. petiolaris*.

A number of perennial sunflowers also can be considered weeds, and, since they can reproduce both by seeds and vegetatively by means of underground stems or roots, some of them are often difficult to eradicate. One of these, the Jerusalem artichoke, is a common weed in the northeastern United States. Blue weed (*H. ciliaris*), an unusual-looking little sunflower so named because of the bluish cast to its leaves, has been a serious agricultural pest in the Southwest. Plants of this species produce roots that may reach several feet in length. In ordinary cultivation or plowing the root may be cut in pieces, and each piece is capable of giving rise to a new plant. Hence plowing serves to spread the plant rather than to eliminate it. Various sprays have been used which have brought it under effective control, although they have by no means eliminated it.

Many years ago at the time when the herbicides were being considered the solution to the "weed problem," I wrote an article called "Weeds Are Here to Stay," and I still subscribe to that view. Although the farmer may kill the sunflowers in his fields every year and buildings now occupy parts of cities where sunflowers once flourished, there are still a lot of sunflowers around. It would be foolish to say that the sunflower will be here forever, for the fossil record tells us that the fate of most plants is extinction. However, that day for the sunflower appears to be in the far distant future.

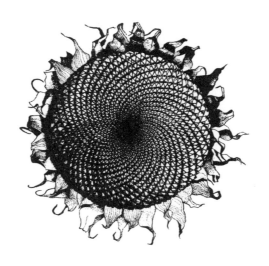

X

The Evolution of Sunflowers

At this point it seems desirable to insert a chapter on evolution, partly so that the reader may better understand some of the material in the chapters to follow.

Few aspects of biology have attracted more attention in the last hundred years or so than the development and the subsequent acceptance of the theory of evolution. The evidence for evolution comes from paleontology, genetics, morphology—in fact, from virtually all fields of biology. The taxonomist has contributed his share. Through his delimitation of species, their distributions, and relationships he provided Darwin, as he provides his biological colleagues today, with the basic facts for the study of evolution.

Neither in his first edition of *The Origin of Species* (1859) nor in subsequent editions was Darwin able to account adequately for a method by which new characters come into existence, and the solution was not provided until early in this century, when gene mutations became understood. It was found that the transmission of characters from one generation to another was dependent upon genes that are carried in chromosomes. The genes, normally stable, pass down exact copies of themselves generation after generation. But on rare occasions a gene fails to duplicate itself exactly, and this changed, or mutated, gene continues to pass down copies of itself. It is such gene mutations that provide the raw material for evolution.

The mutations contribute to the gene pool of a species, and through crossing of individuals the mutations can be recombined in various ways with other genes in the following generations. Some mutants or combinations perhaps result in the death of the individual, but others may produce a better-adapted organism. Thus it can be seen that sexual reproduction is of tremendous importance in evolution, for it allows a continual reshuffling of the genes.

It is at this stage of reproduction that natural selection, the central thesis of Darwin's evolutionary theory, enters the picture. Those plants with favorable mutations are able to produce more descendants than those lacking them. This differential reproduction then guides the course of evolution. As a result of mutation, recombination, and natural selection there may be a gradual change in the composition of a population of a species from generation to generation. This change is organic evolution. It has allowed the common sunflower to produce many wild races adapted to a great variety of environmental conditions.

The giant cultivated sunflower can be postulated to have developed in the same manner, with one significant exception: natural selection has been largely replaced by artificial selection, or selection by man. The statement is sometimes made that cultivation by man changes a plant, but any permanent change still involves mutation. Once man brings a plant under his care, mutations still occur at random. Often, however, mutations that would not stand a chance of surviving under natural conditions are nursed along by man. Practically all the differences between a cultivated and a wild sunflower are ones that would make the cultivated plant poorly adapted to survive in the wild. The branched wild sunflowers with their many heads tend to produce seed over a long period of time, whereas the seeds of the cultivated plant ripen at one time. If this single head fails to be pollinated or is damaged in some way, the plant will fail to produce seeds. The chaffy bracts that partly embrace the individual sunflower achenes in the head tend to spread apart in wild sunflowers, and a bird alighting on the head or the wind may shake some of the achenes to the ground, whereas in the cultivated sunflower the bracts tightly embrace the achenes, and the achenes do not fall out readily—an advantage to man, who would like to harvest all the achenes in a head at one time but a disadvantage to reproduction in the wild. The larger size and the light color of the achene coats of the many cultivated varieties also would probably be a disadvantage to the plant in a natural setting. The darker and speckled colors and the smaller size of the achenes of wild sunflowers may help them escape the notice of some animals when they fall to the ground and thus not be eaten. The achene coats of wild sunflowers are thicker and tougher than those of the cultivated varieties. Thus it is easier for man to extract the seed from the latter, but at the same time they are less well protected against the predation of certain insects. The cultivated sunflower seeds have a rapid and even germination, in contrast to those of the wild types, which have a dormancy period so that they will not germinate immediately after maturity. When they germinate, they do so irregularly. Some may remain in the soil and not germinate until the second or third year. It is to the sunflower grower's advantage to have all the seeds he plants germinate at the same time, but such even germination might spell disaster to a wild plant, for all the seedlings might be killed by a late freeze or a flash flood or some other natural disaster.

Artificial selection allowed such monstrosities as the giant sunflower and the corn plant to come into existence, and it is only through man's efforts that they continue to survive, for they would not stand a chance of competing in nature. Darwin, who was well aware of the differences between wild and cultivated plants, applied this knowledge in developing his theory of evolution.

The many races of the common sunflower are members of a single species, and the giant cultivated sunflower is also a member of the same species. There are, however, over fifty different species of sunflowers. How did they originate? To supply an answer, let us consider a hypothetical example. While no one has ever seen a sunflower develop into a new species, there are many lines of evidence that indicate that our hypothesis of their origin is the correct one. The very fact that today we find many sunflowers in various stages of evolution transitional between variety and species is one of them.

Before proceeding further it may be desirable to arrive at a definition of a species. That is no simple matter. Darwin wrote, "No one definition [of a species] has satisfied all naturalists; yet every naturalist knows vaguely what he means when he speaks of a species." The situation is somewhat better today, and, although naturalists still may disagree, the scientists have come closer to reaching an understanding, and it is now realized that species may vary considerably in different groups of organisms. The reader with some acquaintance with different species of a genus knows that the species usually look different. For example, one may have broad leaves with toothed margins, and another may have narrow leaves with smooth margins. Closer examination will usually reveal other differences in the shape of the flowers, and so on. It is true that species generally differ in several characteristics, conspicuously or inconspicuously, but studies in the last quarter century have indicated that even more fundamental is that a species is incapable of free interbreeding with other species in nature. It is this characteristic that allows species to remain distinct even when they grow together.

Let us assume that in the dim geological past a single species of sunflower existed on the North American continent.

This sunflower grew and reproduced. As mutations occurred, it gradually changed, but all members of the species remained potentially able to interbreed with each other. Thus any mutation that would arise could spread throughout the whole population.

Now let us imagine that in time the species range became disrupted in some manner. The formation of a mountain range might be responsible, or seas might come inland to split the sunflower population into two parts, or somehow seeds from sunflowers might be carried a great distance from their parent populations. The sunflowers would then occupy two separate areas, and, if the geographical barrier was great enough, it would be impossible for insects to carry pollen from one area to the other. This separation would result in two interbreeding units of plants instead of one. This would mean that any mutation that arose in one area of the species could not spread to the other. In addition, we might expect the climate in the two areas to be somewhat different, so that one mutation might be favorable in one area, and, even if the same mutation occurred in the other area, it would not have become established. In time with the accumulation of a number of mutations we might expect the sunflowers in the two areas to become somewhat dissimilar in appearance. At the same time internal changes might have taken place. These changes could have affected the physiology so that the species in one area became adapted to a slightly different soil type, or it may have come into bloom either earlier or later than the plants in the other area. Slight changes in the structure of the chromosomes could also have occurred.

If at some later date the geographical barrier broke down and the two separately evolving populations of sunflowers came into contact with each other, they would continue to behave as independently evolving populations if some of the changes that had occurred during their period of isolation prohibited free interbreeding. There would then be two species instead of one. The two species, most likely—but not necessarily—would look different, but more important is the fact that some sort of isolating mechanism would have developed

105

that would have replaced the geographical barrier that had previously separated them.

Prolonged geographical isolation does not always lead to speciation; it is possible for two geographically separated populations never to develop isolating mechanisms to prevent their interbreeding. Neither will such geographical isolation always lead to a difference in the appearance of the plant populations in the two areas. If, for example, the climate is very similar in the two areas, we might expect little or no change in their appearance. Nevertheless, it seems reasonably certain that the most common kind of speciation in cross-fertilizing organisms occurs through a method similar to that outlined above. In short, it may be stated that geographical isolation along with mutation, recombination, and natural selection may lead to the formation of new species.

The great majority of sunflower species appear to have arisen in the manner just described, but this is not the only method of speciation that has occurred in sunflowers. A clue to the second method is provided by an examination of the chromosome number. Most species of sunflowers have thirty-four chromosomes and are known as the diploid species. Five species, the tetraploid species, have twice that number of chromosomes. Seven other species, the hexaploid species, have three times that number. Those species with multiples of the basic number are known as polyploids, and in the last few decades it has become clear that many species of flowering plants have originated through the process of polyploidy, or chromosome doubling.

Polyploidy, which occurs as the result of a failure of a cell wall to form after the chromosomes have divided, can give rise to a new species at a single step. This occurs most frequently in hybrids between species. The new plant with double the number of chromosomes generally produces sterile hybrids if it is crossed with its diploid progenitors. Thus an isolation is established the moment the polyploid comes into existence. This subject will be discussed in more detail in later chapters dealing with some of the polyploid sunflowers.

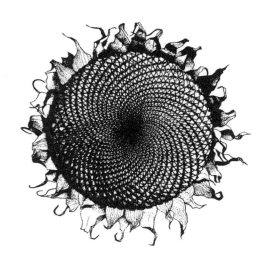

XI

"Nature's Bastards"[1]

SEVERAL of the sunflower's claims to fame have already been discussed. Another one is the propensity of sunflower species to hybridize. The common sunflower is somewhat notorious in this regard, and a great number of perennial species of the eastern United States enter into alliances with other species.

For a long time natural hybrids between species had been regarded as extremely rare, perhaps stemming from the old idea that each species was a special act of creation and hence hybrids between them were unnatural. Only in the last half-century have we arrived at a clear understanding of natural hybridization and its role in evolution. The sunflowers are not alone among flowering plants in their production of hy-

---

[1] With apologies to Milton.

107

brids, for hybridization has been shown to be common in many groups of plants. Violets, for example, which are generally characterized as shy, retiring plants, are extremely promiscuous with other species. More and more hybrids between various animal species, particularly birds and amphibians, have also come to light in recent years.

Before proceeding to some details of sunflower hybridization, a few general remarks on hybrids are in order. The word hybrid has come to have a rather broad meaning. Some would use the word to designate the offspring of two parents that differ in even a single gene. This would make practically all sunflowers—and humans as well—hybrids. Darwin tried to limit the term hybrid to offspring of crosses between species, and that is the sense in which we are using the word in this chapter. The term mongrel was used by Darwin for hybrids within a species.

The mule, the result of a cross between a mare and an ass, has been known since the dawn of history and must rank as the oldest interspecific hybrid on record. Some of the other ancient reports of hybrids, however, are not so trustworthy. At one time it was thought that the mating of a panther and a camel had resulted in the giraffe. The cat-rabbit hybrid is another bit of fantasy from early times that surprisingly is still sometimes reported in popular accounts. Today we know that only very closely related organisms are able to cross with each other. These are usually species of the same genus. Rarely species belonging to closely related genera, as in some orchids, may produce hybrids. One cannot breed a succotash plant by crossing beans and corn.

The mule has been described as an animal "having neither pride of ancestry nor hope of descendants." This statement is more clever than true, for mules on rare occasions have been known to produce offspring, but it does serve to illustrate another feature of hybrids. Frequently hybrids between species are sterile or nearly so, but no generalization can be made, for some hybrids between species may be fertile. In the past some biologists have attempted to define species solely on their inability to produce hybrids with other such groups. Un-

Heads and leaves of *H. annuus* (*left*), *H. debilis* subspecies *cucumerifolius* (*right*), and an artificial hybrid between them (*center*).

fortunately, perhaps, nature refuses to be categorized so simply.

In the previous chapter it was pointed out that species are groups of organisms that could not hybridize freely with other such groups. Such a definition allows occasional hybridization between species. It is also possible that the isolating mechanisms acquired by organisms may break down. We shall see that in sunflowers man has been important in breaking down the barriers between species so that hybrids may at times become established.

As a wild plant and weed our common sunflower has been spread unintentionally by man into new areas, a process that is assumed to have begun in prehistoric times with the Indians and is still going on today. As a result it has come into contact with other species of sunflowers, and in some places interspecific hybridization has taken place.

As the common sunflower moved from its home in the west it encountered the cucumber-leaf sunflower (*H. debilis* sub-

109

species *cucumerifolius*) in eastern Texas. These two sunflowers are quite different—the common sunflower is a tall plant, branching mostly in the upper part, and has rough hairy leaves with a fairly regular saw-tooth margin, whereas the other species is a smaller plant, much branched, with smoother leaves frequently having a jagged edge. There are, in addition, several other less conspicuous characters separating the two species. These two sunflowers also show a striking difference in the kinds of soil in which they grow best. The common sunflower grows in dump heaps or in clay soil but seldom if ever in sandy soils. The cucumber-leaf sunflower, on the other hand, is nearly always found in sandy soils.

When the common sunflower was introduced into Texas, it probably was not well adapted to the new climate in which it found itself. At first it may have been confined to disturbed sites around Indian villages. If they happened to be situated near regions where the cucumber-leaf sunflower grew, cross-pollination could have taken place. Any hybrids formed, although at a serious disadvantage in competing with the species already well adapted to the area, might have a better chance than the ill-adapted common sunflower. In areas where there was a mixture of sandy and clay soil the hybrids might even be at an advantage over the parental species, for hybrids are usually intermediate not only in appearance but also in their soil "preference" and other physiological traits. Although these hybrids have highly reduced fertility, they do produce some good pollen, and this in turn might be carried back to the parent species, producing backcrosses; thus we might expect considerable intercrossing between the species and the hybrids. In time we might expect genes from one species to become incorporated in the other, particularly if they conferred even a slight advantage. Such might well be the case with genes from the cucumber-leaf sunflower passing into the common sunflower. If the latter species was initially poorly adapted to the climate of east Texas, it might acquire valuable genes from the species already well adapted to the area.

The foregoing is a hypothesis, highly speculative in many ways, difficult to disprove and also difficult to prove. Today the common sunflower is widely distributed in eastern Texas, a very successful weed in the cotton country, whereas the cucumber-leaf sunflower remains confined to the sandy soils of the watermelon country and the seashores. When the common sunflowers of east Texas are compared with the same species from the north and west, they are found to differ from them in a number of trivial characteristics: a tendency to branch from the base, occasionally jaggedly cut leaves, small heads and seeds—all characteristics that could have come from the cucumber-leaf sunflower. Moreover, the two species still hybridize in nature in several localities and backcrosses are produced. That these plants found in nature are actually hybrids is well supported by comparison with the many artificial hybrids that have been produced. Thus considerable evidence exists to suggest that there was an introgression of genes from the cucumber-leaf sunflower into the common sunflower.

At this point one may well ask why sunflowers remain as distinct species if they hybridize. Should not hybridization bring about a leveling effect so that eventually we would have only a single variable species? The answer is no, for several reasons. First of all, the hybrids are only partly fertile, and hence their reproductive capacity is lower than that of the parental types. For this reason the hybrids are at a disadvantage—they simply cannot produce as many seeds as the parents. The fact that the two species are adapted to different soil types also helps prevent amalgamation. Presumably certain visible characters are linked to those enabling the plant to grow in a particular habitat. Thus, in general, we would expect plants which look most like the cucumber-leaf sunflower to grow in sandy soil and those like the common sunflower to grow in the heavier soils. That is exactly what we find. Still a third reason is that the two species have slightly different blooming seasons. Obviously the two species must have some overlap in blooming season for hybridization to take place, but the cucumber-leaf sunflower blooms early in the summer, and the common sunflower reaches its peak late in the summer. Thus there is a greater opportunity for plants of each species to cross-pollinate among their own species. These three barriers do not appear strong enough to prevent some gene exchange between species but at the same time are great enough to prevent complete amalgamation.

The common sunflower hybridizes not only with the cucumber-leaf sunflower but with several other annual species as well. In other parts of Texas it is known to hybridize with the silver-leaf sunflower (*H. argophyllus*). In California it hybridizes with a native sunflower of that region, *H. bolanderi*, and in many parts of the west it crosses with *H. petiolaris*. Through backcrossing of the hybrids a trickle of genes may enter the common sunflower, increasing its variability and adaptability. This may help to explain why the common sunflower has become such a wide-ranging and successful weed. On the other hand, hybrids of the common sunflower with the perennial species are unknown in nature because strong barriers to hybridization have developed between the perennial and the annual species (although we shall see that it is sometimes possible to produce artificial hybrids between species of the two groups).

The perennial species hybridize with each other fairly readily. In fact hybridization has been so rampant in some of the perennials that it is almost impossible to classify some individuals, causing no end of confusion to the taxonomist.[2] Some plants that have been named as species have recently been shown to be nothing more than hybrids. Our understanding of the details of these complexities is due in a large

---

[2] The difficulty of identifying sunflowers is well illustrated by the pithy comments of Charles C. Deam, when he was preparing a record of all the plants that occurred in Indiana. In May, 1937, he wrote to Paul Weatherwax, a botanist at Indiana University, commenting on his difficulties in placing his specimens of sunflowers into species: "If I have another attack of *Helianthus*, I am a dead one. I am not sure I shall survive this one. Last night I came across a nondescript. Say man how I hate them. Doubtless sometimes you wish to call someone a mean name. Well, I have found it. Just call him a sunflower. That combines all that is needed. The brutes have no principles, guided by no laws, and seem to [be] free for all." It is now clear that many of the specimens that puzzled Deam were hybrids between species and hence could not be pigeonholed into any one species as he was trying to do.

measure to the recent work of the botanists Dale Smith, Raymond Jackson, Robert Long, and William Martin.

One of the best examples is provided by Smith's analysis of two of our common sunflowers of the eastern United States —*H. divaricatus*, an inconspicuous little plant with opposite, sessile leaves and medium-sized heads which grows at its best in fairly open spots at the edges of woods in what farmers would call very poor soil, and *H. microcephalus*, a small-headed sunflower with alternate, petiolate leaves, generally found in the woods in fairly deep leaf mold. In areas where the forests have been partly cleared, hybrids between the two species are found. An examination of a number of plants revealed that there has been a considerable exchange of genes between the species. The hybrids are seldom found in either dense shade or full sunlight but are at their best in partial shade. The hybrid derivatives, since they can grow in habitats not occupied by the species, have apparently allowed the sunflowers to increase their range.

Just as was true with the annual sunflowers, the hybridization has not resulted in a fusion of the two species but only in a slight blurring of the species boundaries. Instead of sand versus heavier soils, we find here another type of soil preference, as well as a difference in tolerance to sunlight. There is also a slight difference in time of blooming; *H. divaricatus* comes into flower earlier than *H. microcephalus*. The hybrids, unlike those between annual sunflowers, are highly fertile. However, through artificial hybridization experiments it has been found that it is difficult to secure crosses between the two species. Repeated pollinations are necessary to secure hybrid seed. Thus we see once again that species possess several barriers to help them maintain their identity, although inhibition of gene exchange is not complete.

In both the examples given above, it has been shown that man has played an important role—in the common and cucumber-leaf sunflowers, by bringing together two previously geographically separated species, and in the second case, by clearing the forests and thereby providing a new habitat where the hybrids could grow to advantage. Hybridization between species certainly occurred before man appeared on the scene, but today man, through his drastic changing of the environment, is promoting hybridization on a grand scale. Man has caused certain species to become extinct, some he has transformed by intentional hybridization and selection, and others he has changed unintentionally by his disturbance of the environment.

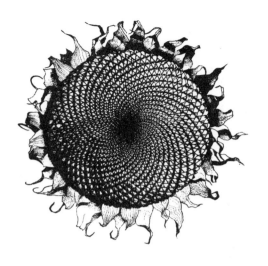

XII

Plant Breeding of Sunflowers

To SAY that the Indians were the first breeders of sunflowers may be stretching a point, for we have no idea how much conscious effort they made to improve the sunflower. It does not seem unreasonable to assume, however, that they did deliberately save and plant seeds from individual plants that had certain desirable characteristics. If this is true, intentional selection could have been practiced at a very early time. Selection of seeds from superior plants continued to be the principal method of plant improvement until recently—and, in fact, is still practiced—but in this century hybridization has become the most important tool of the plant breeder.

Man's earliest experiments at hybridization, however, were carried out in an attempt not to produce better plants but to prove that sex existed in plants. The idea that plants had sex

115

was a radical one when it was first proposed in the seventeenth century. Through hybridization experiments it was shortly demonstrated that a "male element," which we now know as pollen, was necessary to secure seed set in plants.

One of the first to refer to the possible practical application of hybridization was John Bartram, a farmer and botanist, whose famous gardens are still maintained in Philadelphia. Bartram carried out some hybridization in the early part of the eighteenth century, but exactly how much he accomplished is not known. The letter in which he discussed hybridization was not published until a hundred years later, and a prudish editor deleted all his remarks referring to sex in plants.

Although better known for his naming and classification of plants, Linnaeus and some of his students were also interested in hybrids. Linnaeus believed that many vegetables had arisen through hybridization, an idea remarkable for an age in which it was held that each species was an act of special creation. In 1760 he wrote that there was "new employment for botanists to attempt the production of new species of vegetables by scattering the pollen of various plants over various widowed females." Another century was to elapse before much was done along this line, and it was not until this century, with the rediscovery of Mendel's laws of heredity, that the plant breeder gained a real understanding of what he was doing in his work with hybridization.

Both crosses of different forms of the cultivated sunflower with each other and crosses with other species of sunflower have been made in attempts to improve the cultivated sunflower. The earliest recorded work of this nature was done in Russia in 1915, when crosses of the cultivated sunflower were made with the silver-leaf sunflower in an attempt to secure disease resistance in the cultivated plant. Nearly all of the early work on the improvement of the sunflower was done in Russia; even though today there are active breeding programs in many other countries, including the United States, the Soviet Union still continues to have the largest breeding program for sunflowers.

116

The breeding aims in sunflower improvement have been concentrated on increasing oil content, yield, and disease resistance. In an earlier chapter it was pointed out that the Russians had increased the oil content from 28 per cent to 50 per cent. Yields have also been greatly increased.

Perhaps even greater effort has been devoted to securing varieties resistant to the many diseases that plague the crop. This is not unusual for a crop plant, and the plant breeders face an apparently never-ending battle with some of the diseases. For example, once a variety is bred resistant to a rust, the rust in turn may produce new races that can attack the newly created variety. Rust is the most serious disease of sunflowers, and it frequently reduces yields by 20 per cent or more. The sunflower is host to a number of other fungal diseases and viruses as well. These include downy mildew, leaf mottle, leaf spot, black stem, and wilts. The sunflower is also subject to attack by a number of insects, and the sunflower moth often causes extensive losses. Previously it was mentioned that the plant diseases and pests seem to be most numerous in the homeland of a crop, but there is one pest of the sunflower, broomrape, a parasitic flowering plant, that has been known to cause extensive damage among sunflower crops in Europe. It has never appeared in the Americas.

The plant-breeding work in the Soviet Union has involved what I may call superstition for want of a better word, as well as an application of solid genetic principles. In 1937 the direction of agriculture in Russia fell into the hands of T. D. Lysenko, who has been described as an illiterate and fanatical charlatan who did not believe in classical genetics. He recommended certain methods for crop improvement whose value had not been scientifically demonstrated, and the extravagant claims made for the new methods were never substantiated. Finally in 1964, Lysenko fell from power, and the Soviet Union's scientists once more returned to traditional methods, although at times the plant breeders still employ certain practices such as "vegetative hybridization" (grafting), in order to secure wide crosses, and other procedures whose value is questionable. Since the oil content of the sunflower increased

A sunflower-breeding trial plot at All-Union Research Institute of Oil Crops, Krasnodar, U.S.S.R. Courtesy of N. Dvoryadkin.

during Lysenko's tenure, it seems apparent that some plant breeders, while paying lip service to Lysenko's methods, were at the same time practicing the kind of scientific work known to give beneficial results.

One of the notable successes in the plant-breeding work in the Soviet Union has come about through the incorporation of genes from the Jerusalem artichoke (*H. tuberosus*) into the cultivated sunflower. The Jerusalem artichoke is a perennial, polyploid sunflower. Although crosses between *H. annuus* and *H. tuberosus* have never been found in nature, it is fairly easy to secure a few seeds from artificial crosses of the two species. Although the resulting F_1 hybrid usually shows a high degree of sterility, it is possible to increase fertility by backcrossing.

Above: the Mammoth Russian sunflower; *below:* an abnormal specimen of the same sunflower, in which leafy bracts have replaced the central disk flowers.

The common sunflower, ancestor of our giant cultivated sunflower.

The double-flowered form of the common sunflower.

A row of red sunflowers grows beside a row of silver-leaf sunflowers (*Helianthus argophyllus*) not yet in flower.

Above: the red sunflower, chestnut type; *below:* the red sunflower, plum type.

Above: H. × *multiflorus; below:* a showy sunflower (*H.* × *laetiflorus*), a widely grown perennial ornamental.

The Jerusalem artichoke (*H. tuberosus*), with other perennial species in the background.

The orange, or Mexican, sunflower (*Tithonia rotundifolia*).

By continual backcrossing followed by selection, the Russians secured "group immunity" to rust, downy mildew, sunflower wilt, and sclerotinia disease in the cultivated sunflowers and at the same time increased the oil content and yield. It is of interest to note here that the Russians have been willing to send seeds of their superior varieties to plant breeders in other countries.

The wild form of the common sunflower has also been a source of disease resistance. In many plants it has been found that the wild ancestor of a cultivated plant frequently is a good source for disease-resistance genes, for if a wild form survives, it is likely to have some disease resistance. A gene for rust resistance has been found in wild populations of sunflowers in Texas and has been incorporated into a number of cultivated strains. The Indian races of the cultivated sunflower have not been the source of valuable genes for the plant breeder, but few of them have yet been intensively tested.

Some years ago it was realized that a significant breakthrough in sunflower yields would come with the production of an F_1 intervarietal hybrid sunflower that could be grown commercially to exploit the tremendous vigor and consequently the increased yields found in first-generation hybrids. This had already been demonstrated in a number of crops, notably corn. In fact, virtually all the corn grown in the United States today is hybrid.

The securing of hybrid seed on a large scale is a far more difficult problem in sunflowers than in corn. In the latter the male and female flowers are produced in separate structures, which made the production of hybrid seed a relatively simple matter. The two varieties of corn to be crossed were grown side by side in rows. The male flowers in one variety were removed by detasseling, and as a result all the seeds it produced resulted from pollination by the other variety. The seeds could then be sold to the farmer, who would grow the hybrids in his field the next summer.

The sunflower, on the other hand, has small, bisexual flowers; emasculating them is not as simple as detasseling

Normal and male sterile sunflowers. The pollen on the normal head (*left*) can be seen as white dots on the outer circles of disk flowers.

corn and is a very time- consuming operation, totally impractical on a field scale. However, even if emasculation is not practiced, when two varieties are grown together it is possible with some varieties to secure a fairly high percentage of hybrids. This was done with sunflowers, although the results were not always satisfactory, and the breeders realized that the only practical method of securing hybrid seeds would be through mass sterilization of the male flowers of one of the varieties.

The ideal solution would be to find a genetic factor, and this would not be a gene carried in the chromosomes since there would be segregation for the character in the progeny. What would be necessary would be a genetic factor that was carried not in the chromosomes but in the cytoplasm of the cells. Similar cytoplasmic factors causing male sterility had already been found in a number of plants, including corn, eliminating the necessity of detasseling the corn to produce hybrids. It is now possible to grow two varieties of corn together, with one variety carrying a cytoplasmic factor for male sterility that inhibits pollen development. Male fertility can be restored in the next generation by utilizing a strain containing a fertility-restoring gene so that the hybrids grown by the farmer produce normal pollen.

Thus a search was on for a sunflower with a cytoplasmic factor that would inhibit the production of functional pollen. Such a plant might turn up almost anywhere—in a field of wild or cultivated plants or in a hybrid between species. Both Eric Putt, one of Canada's outstanding plant breeders of sunflowers, and I discovered male sterile plants, whose sterility unfortunately proved to be controlled by genes rather than by cytoplasmic factors. While such plants were of some interest, they were, as we both knew, not the solution to producing commercial hybrid sunflowers. In 1969 a French worker, Patrice Leclercq, reported the discovery of cytoplasmic male sterility in hybrids of *H. annuus* with *H. petiolaris*. Later Murray Kinman, of the United States Department of Agriculture, who for many years had been this country's foremost breeder of sunflowers, announced the discovery of fertility-restoring genes.

As of this writing, hybrid sunflowers are being grown on an experimental basis and have already shown tremendous increases in yields, ranging to 30 per cent over that of standard varieties. The introduction of hybrids into commercial production appears to offer a great future for sunflowers.

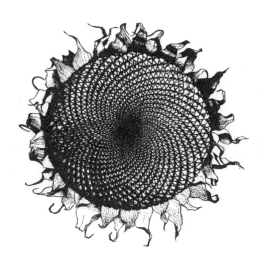

XIII

Horse Bouquet[1]

The sunflower 'tis rank and coarse
'Twould make a lovely bouquet for a horse.

—Anonymous

As a FIELD CROP in the United States sunflowers do not appear to be offering much competition to corn, and the marigolds hardly need worry that the sunflower will usurp their place among the ornamentals. In grandmother's time they were a great favorite, and thousands of sunflowers are still grown yearly as ornamentals. They seem to be more appreciated in Europe than in their homeland—the old story of the commonplace holding little appeal.

---

[1] I once submitted an article under this title to a garden magazine. Before publication the editor changed the title to "Know Your Annual Sunflowers."

131

This bouquet contains various ornamental types of the common sunflower.

In spite of their ungainliness, sunflowers have a number of good points. Given a sunny location, they are easy to grow. They are not too fussy about the type of soil, and they do not require much attention. Their height is a definite advantage if one wants to camouflage a garbage pail or a privy. Although you would not find them in a florist shop being sold as corsages, they make good cut flowers, and they have served as subjects for many artists.

When the common sunflower first went to Europe, it was grown as a curiosity. The Europeans were fascinated by this gaudy plant that could grow to such great heights in a space of a few months. Other kinds of sunflowers were sent to Europe during the sixteenth and seventeenth centuries, including new varieties of the giant sunflower, as well as various wild species. These were unlike any native plants of the Old World and soon became prized as garden ornamentals. The best-known ornamental, as well as the oldest, is our old friend,

Double form of the common sunflower.

the common sunflower (*H. annuus*). Actually the common sunflower includes a number of varieties in addition to the cultivated and wild sunflowers which have been the subject of earlier chapters. Among the most attractive are the so-called double sunflowers, which have heads that look like giant chrysanthemums. Many people fail to realize that they are sunflowers. The double sunflower owes its unusual appearance to the fact that the disk flowers have become elongated and somewhat quilled. It is apparently very old, for it is illustrated in the herbals, and the mutation which caused it apparently occurred in the first hundred years after the sunflower reached Europe. One of the best of the doubles, Sun Gold, was introduced in the late 1940's and has the virtue of being shorter (three to five feet) than most of the common sunflowers. A still shorter variety, Teddy Bear, has been introduced more recently, but to me it is less ornamental than Sun Gold. When a sunflower becomes too short, it loses some of its most distinctive character.

Mr. and Mrs. T. D. A. Cockerell in their sunflower garden, Boulder, Colorado, 1916.

The red sunflower, unlike the other cultivated sunflowers, arose in recent times and its history is precisely known. The name T. D. A. Cockerell, an Englishman who went to Colorado for his health in 1887, will always be associated with the red sunflower. Although primarily a student of insects, he also had a keen interest in plants and listened with amazement to the story his wife told him one summer day in 1910. That morning not far from their house she had seen what she thought was a red butterfly on one of the many sunflowers that grew along the roadside. She stood watching it, and when it did not fly away she went closer to investigate. To her surprise it was not a butterfly but a red sunflower. Immediately the Cockerells realized that it might be a plant of considerable importance to science, particularly to horticulture. They carefully dug it up and transplanted it in their yard.

Fortunately, Cockerell was well acquainted with the laws of genetics, which had been rediscovered only a few years previously. Sunflowers were cross-pollinated, he knew, and a yellow-flowered plant would have to serve as the pollen parent

This red sunflower was grown by Cockerell in 1916.

of the seeds secured from the red plant. The resulting hybrids would have to be intercrossed, and from these plants he might hope to recapture some plants like the original one in the next generation. So with considerable patience the Cockerells crossed plants until they secured a true-breeding red sunflower. They sold seeds to Sutton and Sons, an English seed company, and eventually the red sunflower spread around the world much as had the giant sunflower earlier. When the Cockerells visited Russia in 1932, they were pleased to see the red sunflower being cultivated in a public park near the Black Sea. But their pleasure was short-lived, for, upon inquiring about the source of their sunflower, the director of the park told them, "Madam, this is not your sunflower but the red sunflower of the Red Army."

The inheritance of the red ray color in the sunflower is of some interest. Two major genes control the color—one operates to produce a reddish pigment, and a second factor controls the production of the orange-yellow color characteristic of wild sunflowers. When dominant genes of both of these are present, a chestnut color is produced; when the red gene is present in combination with the recessive forms of the orange-yellow gene, a plum-colored ray results; if the recessives of the red factor are present with a dominant orange gene, the wild type appears; and if the recessives of both genes occur together, the ray flowers are a pale yellow in color. Thus four main color types can appear—chestnut, plum, orange-yellow, and primrose. Other factors operate to control the intensity of the color and various pattern effects. Today we have not only the four main types but maroon- and wine-colored ones and some streaked with red and gold as well. Although the mutation that produced the red color may have occurred more than once, it is probable that all the red sunflowers grown today are derived from the single wild plant which appeared spontaneously among a group of wild plants along a roadside in Colorado. Cockerell, who always published his scientific discoveries immediately because he thought death was imminent, lived to the age of eighty-two. His interest in sunflowers continued to the very end of his life, and I enjoyed a lively cor-

The silver-leaf sunflower, a young plant viewed from the top.

respondence with him about the subject for a number of years.

Some time ago I obtained a red double sunflower, but it is not offered in the trade. By crossing the red sunflower with the double, one obtains a semidouble form with a rustlike color. By crossing two of these plants together, one obtains a great array of types—some very much like the red sunflower, some almost exactly like the double parent, and a few that are red double forms. However, most of the persons who have seen this sunflower do not feel that it is as beautiful as either parent; one went so far as to suggest the name Dust Mop for it.

Two other annual sunflowers are less widely grown as garden flowers, but in some ways both are superior to the common sunflower. The silver-leaf sunflower (*H. argophyllus*), native to coastal Texas, has leaves and stems covered with long silky white hairs that make it a striking plant even when it is not in flower. One does not see it grown very often, however, and in my search for seeds of it a few years ago I wrote to the Bodger Seed Company of Los Angeles, which had always carried a large number of sunflowers. They reported that they no longer handled this species. A few months later,

A mutant of the silver-leaf sunflower in which the normal flat rays have been replaced by quill-like structures.

however, I received a letter from Bodger enclosing seeds of this species and explaining that they had been sent to him from a collector in Australia who had found the plant growing "wild" there. These "wild" plants had escaped from cultivation as sunflowers frequently do. Perhaps one reason this species has become neglected is that in many areas it flowers so late that it is caught by frost before it is in full bloom, a fate that meets many southern plants when they are grown in the north. Early-flowering types of *H. argophyllus* are now known, however. Interesting mutant types are also known in which the normal flat yellow rays are replaced by short quill-like structures tipped with red or are completely lacking. These are perhaps better regarded as novelties than as ornamentals. Although both this species and the next to be discussed grow naturally only in sandy soil, they do very well under cultivation in a wide variety of soil types.

Many persons fail to realize that the cucumber-leaf sunflower (*H. debilis* subspecies *cucumerifolius*), another native of Texas, is a sunflower and not some kind of black-eyed

Italian white variety of the cucumber-leaf sunflower.

Susan. The mistaken impression results from the fact that this plant is smaller and more delicate than most sunflowers, which of course in some ways makes it a much better plant for the garden. One form of this sunflower, Italian White, has rays that are a cream or pale primrose color, and although it adds variety to the garden, it is not as striking as the more typical form with the deep orange-yellow rays. Other forms are known with rays of apricot or coral color. A double form of this species appeared as a mutant in my garden a few years ago and appears to hold some promise as an ornamental. However, it is characterized by being almost sterile, and thus far it has been impossible to secure a pure line since the few seeds that it sets have to be secured by using semidouble sorts as the male parent.

Closely related to the cucumber-leaf sunflower is the beach sunflower. (*H. debilis* subspecies *debilis*) of coastal Florida (Kansas and Texas by no means have a monopoly on sunflowers). This flower, which, unlike most sunflowers grows nearly prostrate, may in a sense be considered the aristocrat

Maximilian's sunflower.

of the genus, for it grows only on the best beaches in Florida from Marineland to Miami Beach. Its use as an ornamental is largely limited to Florida, where some people transplant it from the beach to their yards.

The perennial sunflowers have not done as well as the annuals when it comes to ornamentals, but several of them have made their way into the perennial border where a tall plant is needed, and some of them have graceful plumes of fifty or more heads, such as Maximilian's sunflower and the willow-leaf sunflower. *H. maximiliani,* named for Maximilian of Wied, a Prussian prince, who collected it in his travels in the United States from 1832 to 1834, is native to the Great Plains and does well in a variety of garden soils. This species has large golden yellow heads which are clustered close to the stem. The plants are generally five to seven feet tall and come into bloom in late summer or autumn after most other perennials in the garden have started to fade. The grayish leaves of

A hybrid of Maximilian's sunflower and the saw-tooth sunflower.

The willow-leaf sunflower.

these plants also make it attractive in its vegetative state. Hybrids which have been made between Maximilian's sunflower and a related species, *H. grosseserratus*, appear to hold great promise for being a better ornamental than either of the parents.

The willow-leaf sunflower, *H. salicifolius*, is somewhat of a giant, reaching heights of six to ten or even twelve feet, but in spite of its height it is an extremely graceful plant. The very narrow, willowlike leaves lend it a special distinction, and the numerous small heads with their yellow rays and dark center appear in autumn. As a wild plant it is for the most part restricted to the Ozark region.

Another perennial sunflower, *H. multiflorus*, is a double sort that is sometimes confused with a chrysanthemum or dahlia.

H. multiflorus.

This sunflower, certainly one of the most beautiful in the whole genus, sets no seed and has to be propagated by vegetative means. The early history of this plant can be traced almost exactly from the descriptions left us by the herbalists in the sixteenth and seventeenth centuries.

Apparently the first description of the plant is in the herbal of Jacob Theodor (1591), or Tabernaemontanus, as he called himself, where it was designated *Corona solis minor foemina*, or "lesser female" sunflower. In 1597 John Gerard, the English botanist, was possibly the first to note the sterility of the plant, stating that "the seed as yet I have not observed." In 1623, the Swiss Gaspard Bauhin reported it, under the name *Helenium Indicum ramosum*, in Spain, Italy, and Germany. If his observation was correct, it apparently attained a very wide distribution in a short space of time, particularly so for a plant that was not spread by seed. Robert

H. decapetalus, one of the parents of *H. multiflorus*.

Morison, writing from England in 1699, clearly stated that the plant, which he called *Chrysanthemum americanum majus perenne*, did not mature seed.

In the middle of the next century the great Swedish naturalist Linnaeus gave it the name *Helianthus multiflorus*, and one of his students made the first study of its origin, concluding that it was a hybrid between *H. annuus* and *H. tuberosus*, which as we shall see, is not too far from the truth. Asa Gray, the father of American botany and a great authority on composites, considered *H. multiflorus* merely a variety of the eastern woodland sunflower *H. decapetalus*, but he commented in 1884 that it was "known only in cultivation." In a special horticultural conference devoted to asters and sunflowers held at Chiswick, England, in 1891, D. DeWar disagreed with Gray and stated that there was a wide gap between *H. decapetalus* and *H. multiflorus* and that, in fact, they were as distinct as any two species of sunflowers. The most significant statements to come out of the conference, however, were those made by a Reverend C. Wolley Dod at the conclusion of DeWar's talk. He agreed that the botanists' account of *H. multiflorus* was not satisfactory. There was, indeed, a wide gap between it and *H. decapetalus*. Perhaps, he suggested, it was a hybrid of *H. decapetalus* and *H. annuus*. The latter was the only other sunflower known with double forms, and moreover *H. multiflorus* was sterile. "Could anyone say that he had ever raised a seedling from it? Perhaps we may some day have more certain evidence by the suggested cross being erected artificially." However, in spite of this discussion Liberty Hyde Bailey, the American authority on cultivated plants, in 1923 followed Gray and considered it a variety of *H. decapetalus*.

Such was the state of affairs when Dale Smith and I began our studies on the plant, although it might be pointed out that we were not aware of the work of Linnaeus' student and the comments of Rev. Dod until we were well along with our investigations. An important clue to the origin of the plant was first provided by a look at the chromosomes. Sunflower species are known with two, four, or six sets of chromosomes, always an even number. However, *H. multiflorus* was found to have three sets of chromosomes, which suggested at once that it might be a hybrid between a plant with two sets and a plant with four sets of chromosomes. The triploid nature of this plant would also explain the sterility since balanced chromosome sets are ordinarily needed for fertility. *H. decapetalus* has four sets of chromosomes and could very well be one parent. The search began for the second parent. *H. multiflorus* differs from *H. decapetalus* in having larger heads, broader and more deeply toothed leaves, and other morphological features pointing toward the common sunflower, *H. annuus*, which also has the prerequisite two sets of chromosomes. Accordingly, attempts were made to secure hybrids between the two species, and a few were obtained, which, while not exactly like *H. multiflorus*, were so similar that there could be little doubt concerning the origin of this "species."[2]

---

[2] Since this plant is thought to be of hybrid origin, its name should formally be given as *Helianthus* × *multiflorus*.

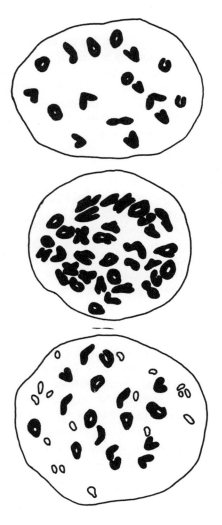

Chromosomes of (*top*) *H. annuus*, (*middle*) *H. decapetalus*, and (*bottom*) *H. multiflorus*. The 34 chromosomes of *H. annuus* form 17 pairs; the 68 chromosomes of *H. decapetalus* form 34 pairs; in *H. multiflorus* 34 of the chromosomes are paired and 17 (unshaded) remain unpaired. These chromosomes are drawn from stained squashes of young anthers in which the pollen is developing and are shown magnified about 1,200 times.

A study of history at this point provides an interesting anomaly. We have seen that *H. multiflorus* was first reported in Europe at the end of the sixteenth century. One of its presumed parents, *H. annuus*, was, of course, well established in Europe by this time. The other supposed parent, however, *H. decapetalus*, was not definitely reported from Europe until over one hundred years later. Since it seems most unlikely that the hybrid first appeared in North America, where it still is not known to occur naturally, and was then taken to Europe, it is probable that *H. decapetalus* was introduced into Europe long before it was formally listed by botanists.

In addition to the double forms of *H. multiflorus*, single forms are also known, and some question exists whether they had independent origins or whether the double form arose directly from the single. The double form is by far the more ornamental; but for comments on this and the use of the plant, let us turn to the words of an eighteenth-century horticulturist, Philip Miller. Miller was Fellow of the Royal Society, gardener to the Worshipful Companies of Apothecaries at their Botanic Garden in Chelsea, and member of the Botanic Garden at Florence, Italy. His work, *The Gardeners Dictionary*,[3] is certainly one of the outstanding garden books, as well as an outstanding taxonomic work of the eighteenth century:

The second sort [of sunflower, *H. multiflorus*], which is most common in the English gardens, is the largest and most valuable flower, and is very proper furniture for large borders in great gardens, as also for bosquets of large growing plants, or to intermix in small quarters with shrubs, or in walks under trees, where few other plants will thrive; it is also a great ornament to gardens within the city, where it grows in defiance of the smoke, better than

---

[3] The full title is *The Gardeners Dictionary: containing the best and newest methods of cultivating and improving the kitchen, fruit, flower garden, and nursery; as also for performing the practical arts of agriculture: including the managing of vineyards, according to present practice of the most skillful vignerons in the several wine companies in* Europe. *Together with directions for propagating and improving, from real practice and experience, all sorts of timber trees.* This quotation is taken from the 8th edition (London, 1768).

most other plants; and for its long continuance in flower, deserves a place in most gardens, for the sake of its flowers for basons, etc. to adorn halls and chimneys, in a season when we are at a loss for other flowers. It begins flowering in July, and continues until October; there is a variety of this with very double flowers, which is now become so common in the English gardens, as to have almost banished the single sort from hence.

Another reason why many people grow sunflowers in their garden is not for ornament but as a source of bird food. Many birds will visit the garden in late summer to enjoy the sunflower harvest. Birds like sunflower seeds so much that they sometimes constitute a menace to farmers who are growing the sunflowers for seed, and the plant breeder has worked hard to eliminate those cultivated types which hold the mature head erect, forming a perfect bird table. For several summers now my field of wild sunflowers has supported a whole flock of goldfinches. They appear in late June and take the seeds from the head even before they have had time to ripen. Later on the turtledoves appear and walk down between the shady rows of sunflowers searching for seeds on the ground. It is absolutely necessary that I cover any heads from which I hope to harvest seeds later. Many persons, of course, save the seeds from the larger type or buy them to feed the birds during the winter.

Although the sunflower cannot compete with its relatives the dahlias, the marigolds, the zinnias, and the chrysanthemums, it still brings a touch of beauty and uniqueness to the garden. In the slum areas around our larger cities, where it thrives as a weed, it is greatly appreciated. Although a yard may be bare from the playing of children, if a sunflower dares to come up it is frequently protected by a few sticks and string and allowed to unfold its leafy rays to the sun, as the poets say. Perhaps it would make a better symbol for the common man than for the knight for which Swinburne chose it.

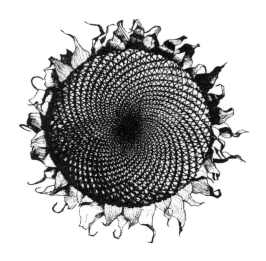

XIV

The Ornamental Sunflowers: A Key to Species, Descriptions, Cultural Requirements, and Production of Hybrids

I dreamt I set a sunflower
And red as blood it grew—

But such a sunflower never
Bloomed beneath the sun.
—Christina G. Rossetti

THERE ARE seventeen species of sunflowers that might be considered cultivated plants, although some of them are seldom seen in gardens today, and still fewer are handled by nurseries and seedsmen. In order to facilitate identification of these cultivated sunflowers, a key and brief descriptions are given in this chapter. Sunflowers are notoriously difficult to identify, and frequently a specialist is needed to make an exact identification of a particular plant. Not the least of the difficulties sometimes is to decide whether or not a particular plant is a true *Helianthus*.

No one characteristic will always serve to distinguish a sunflower from a member of a closely related genus. Although sunflowers are, in general, large, coarse plants, some are rather small and not indelicate. At the same time there are some large coarse plants with sunflowerlike heads that are not true sunflowers. The ray flowers in sunflowers are nearly always some shade of yellow—a very few have reddish rays —but the rays are never a true orange in color so this eliminates the orange, or Mexican, sunflower (*Tithonia rotundifolia*), a garden ornamental from Central America and Mexico which is sometimes confused with the sunflower. The ray flowers in sunflowers, moreover, never produce seeds; this fact aids in separating the sunflowers from the genus *Heliopsis*, or false sunflower, which, although not a close relative, is often thought by the novice to be a sunflower. The bracts (phyllaries), or small leaflike structures which surround the head, are always in two or more series in sunflowers. Each individual disk flower is subtended by a chaffy bract which is perhaps best observed in the dried-up heads. Finally the achene bears two (seldom more) small scales, the pappus, at its summit which fall off readily in the mature fruit. Although it may seem a trivial character, whether or not these scales persist on the achene or are deciduous is one of the most important diagnostic characters separating *Helianthus* from its closest relative, *Viguiera*. Since *Viguiera* is not known in cultivation, however, this character is of consequence only when dealing with wild plants.

The key which follows always gives two choices. For example, the first choice involves deciding whether the disk flowers in the center of the head are red or yellow. If the head is red, one then selects the first part of the key and disregards the part under numeral II. One next has to choose between A and AA. If the particular plant being keyed is a perennial, the name will fall somewhere under A. Thus, by selecting the correct choices, one eventually comes to a name for the plant he is trying to identify. He then can turn to the descrip-

The orange sunflower (*Tithonia rotundifolia*).

tions of the plants that follow the key and check his plant against the description given there. In both the key and the descriptions technical language has been avoided as far as possible, but it is not always possible or desirable to do so. Hence the reader may have to resort to a dictionary to look up certain words. Keying is not a simple matter, particularly in sunflowers, since nearly all sunflower species are extremely variable. It can be seen from the descriptions of the plants that size, in particular, varies greatly for a given species. Some of the size differences and other differences depend on environmental conditions, whether the plants are grown in good soil or poor soil, for example, and some of it is due to genetic differences existing within the species.

For each species the scientific name is followed by (1) the name, or the abbreviation of the name, of the man who first named the species, (2) a translation of the Latin species name, (3) the common name, if one is known, (4) a brief description of the plant, emphasizing the most important diagnostic characteristics, (5) the geographical range of the species in nature, and (6) the months during which the particular species is most commonly found in flower. An asterisk is used to indicate those species which I consider most desirable for the garden.

151

KEY TO SPECIES

I. Disk flowers red or purple
  A. Plants perennials, leaves alternate or opposite
    B. Leaves long and narrow (linear to linear-lanceolate);
      margins without teeth or obscurely toothed
      C. Stems smooth; plants usually over 6 feet tall in cul-
        tivation—

                                          17. *H. salicifolius*
      CC. Stems short-hairy; plants seldom over 6 feet tall—
                                       18. *H. angustifolius*
   BB. Leaves broader (lanceolate to ovate); margins frequent-
      ly toothed
      D. Plants green, sparingly to moderately pubescent;
        rhizomes or basal buds present
        E. Leaves more numerous near base of plant, dark
          green, ovate to ovate-lanceolate—

                                  7. *H. atrorubens*
        EE. Stems leafy, leaves light green, usually lanceo-
          late—

                                  8. *H. rigidus*
     DD. Plants almost white; densely pubescent; from deep
        tap root, no rhizomes or basal buds present—

                                  5. *H. niveus*
 AA. Plants annuals, upper leaves always alternate
      F. Leaves and stems grayish-white because of the pres-
        ence of long, soft, silky hairs—

                                2. *H. argophyllus*
     FF. Leaves and stems green; pubescence usually harsh
      G. Phyllaries ovate to ovate-lanceolate; conspicuous-
        ly ciliate on margins; disk usually over 2 inches
        broad—

                                  1. *H. annuus*
     GG. Phyllaries lanceolate, usually not ciliate on mar-
        gins; disk usually less than 2 inches broad
        H. Center of disk with conspicuous white hairs;
          leaves not cordate at base, bluish-green—

                                  4. *H. petiolaris*
        HH. Center of head without white hairs; leaves fre-
          quently cordate, dark green—

                                  3. *H. debilis*

II. Disk flowers yellow

    i. Plant annual, disk usually 3 inches or more in diameter—

           1. *H. annuus*

    ii. Plant perennial, disk usually less than 3 inches in diameter

      J. Leaves sessile or with very short petioles

        K. Leaves ovate, opposite, strictly sessile—

           13. *H. mollis*

        KK. Leaves lanceolate, upper alternate usually with short petioles

          L. Stem hairs spreading, leaves generally flat—

           15. *H. giganteus*

          LL. Stem hairs appressed, leaves generally somewhat conduplicate—

           14. *H. maximiliani*

      JJ. Leaves with evident petioles

        M. Leaves mostly basal, those on stem much reduced in size—

           6. *H. occidentalis*

        MM. Stems leafy

          N. Leaves lanceolate, middle stem leaves alternate, roots thickened

            O. Stems glabrous and glaucous—

           16. *H. grosseserratus*

            OO. Stem hairy (see 14 and 15 above)

          NN. Leaves ovate or ovate-lanceolate, middle stem leaves usually opposite; roots not thickened

            P. Heads usually double, plants not producing seed—

           12. *H.* × *multiflorus*

            PP. Heads usually single, producing seed

              Q. Stems nearly glabrous or sparingly hairy, rays pale yellow—

           11. *H. decapetalus*

              QQ. Stems rough or hairy, rays deep yellow

                R. Leaves rough and shiny; tubers generally lacking—

            9. *H.* × *laetiflorus*

                RR. Leaves hairy and dull; tubers usually present—

            10. *H. tuberosus*

1. *H. annuus* L. (annual). Common Sunflower. Large, coarse annual, 4–12 feet tall; stems rough-hairy; leaves usually over 5 inches long, ovate, cordate at base; phyllaries ovate or ovate-lanceolate, abruptly attenuate; heads much larger than in other species. Late July to August. Three main "varieties," or subspecies, may be recognized:

a. *H. annuus* subsp. *lenticularis* (Dougl.) Ckll. (lenticular). The "wild" sunflower of western North America, generally somewhat smaller and less ornamental than the following two varieties. The original "red" sunflower arose in this variety.

b. *H. annuus* subsp. *annuus*. The "weed" sunflower of the central and eastern United States. Most of the cultivated ornamentals apparently should be referred to this variety, including the "red" forms now in cultivation. The double sunflower, of which the cultivar Sun Gold is one of the finest, also belongs here.

c. *H. annuus* var. *macrocarpus* (DC.) Ckll. (large-fruited). The giant-headed unbranched sunflowers. Numerous named cultivars or varieties are known, based primarily on achene markings and height. Mammoth Russian with its gray-striped achene is still the type most commonly seen in the United States.

2. *H. argophyllus* T. & G. (silver leaf). Silver-Leaf Sunflower. Annual, differing from *H. annuus* subsp. *lenticularis* chiefly in having dense, silky, grayish-white pubescence on the stems, leaves, and phyllaries. Sandy soil. Native to east Texas and established in some areas of Florida. Sept.–Oct.

3. *H. debilis* Nutt. (weak). Annual, decumbent or erect, 1–5 feet tall; stem glabrous and sparingly hispid; often purple- and green-mottled; leaves mostly alternate, deltoid-ovate to lance-ovate, 2–5 inches long, cuneate to cordate at base; phyllaries lanceolate; heads smaller than in the first two species. Sandy soil, Florida to east Texas. July–Aug. Several naturally occurring races of this species are recognized, the following two of which are most common as ornamentals:

a. *H. debilis* subsp. *debilis*. Beach Sunflower. This is the prostrate form of the species, occurring along the Atlantic coast of Florida, where it blooms almost year round. Its shiny green leaves and small, numerous dark-centered heads make it an attractive ornamental. So far its cultivation seems to be limited to Florida, where it is sometimes transplanted to yards.

b. *H. debilis* subsp. *cucumerifolius* (T. & G.) Heiser (cucumber-leaf). Cucumber-leaf Sunflower. An erect form from eastern

This close-up of the head of a prairie sunflower (*H. petiolaris*) shows the distinctive white center.

Texas. A number of different ray colors are known for this variety —primrose, pink, and orange-yellow. Next to *H. annuus*, the most commonly cultivated annual sunflower. Known in cultivation for around one hundred years.

4. *H. petiolaris* Nutt. (petioled) Prairie Sunflower. Annual, 2–5 feet tall; leaves alternate, deltoid-ovate to lanceolate, 2–5 inches long, usually bluish-green in color; phyllaries lanceolate or ovate-lanceolate; center of disk whitish owing to presence of long hairs on chaff. Great Plains to the Rockies. June–Aug. Thomas Nuttall, who first described this plant in 1821, commented that it should make a fine ornamental, although so far there has been no serious attempt to use it as such. Its extremely long "flower" stalks make it ideal for cut flowers.

5. *H. niveus* (Benth.) Brandegee (snowy). Annual or perennial from tap root, 3–6 feet tall; leaves, stems, and phyllaries densely clothed with appressed hairs, giving the whole plant a white color; leaves alternate, deltoid-ovate. From early spring to throughout most of the year. This is a desert species of the southwestern United States and Mexico. Apparently it is quite rare, and there is no record that it is grown as an ornamental, although some of its varieties are among the most beautiful sunflowers.

H. niveus on sand dunes in Baja California.

6. *H. occidentalis* Riddell (western). Few-Leaf Sunflower. Perennial from long slender rhizomes, 2–4 feet tall; stems glabrous or nearly so; leaves mostly near the base of the plant, oblanceolate to spatulate, 4–12 inches long, usually entire; petiole barely winged; heads few and small; phyllaries linear-lanceolate. Ohio to Minnesota south to the Ozarks. July–Sept. Little seen in cultivation today. The heads are too small to make it a good ornamental.

7. *H. atrorubens* L. (dark red). Darkeye Sunflower. Perennial from short rhizome, 2–5 feet tall; stem rough-hairy; leaves ovate-spatulate to 10 inches long, usually somewhat serrate; petiole strongly winged; phyllaries oblong with rounded mucronate tips. North Carolina and Kentucky south to Georgia and Mississippi. Aug.–Oct.

8. *H. rigidus* (Cass.) Desf. (stiff). Stiff Sunflower. Perennial from thick rhizome, 3–6 feet tall; stem rough; leaves linear-lanceolate to ovate-lanceolate to 10 inches long, stiff and thick; petiole slightly winged; heads usually larger than in previous species; phyllaries ovate, obtuse. Michigan to Minnesota south to

156

The showy sunflower (*H.* × *laetiflorus*), one of the most widely cultivated of the perennial sunflowers.

These ashy sunflowers are bagged for making crosses.

northern Texas. Aug.–Sept. This species grades into the next, although in general the disk color is red in *H. rigidus*, whereas it is always yellow in *H.* × *laetiflorus*.

9. *H.* × *laetiflorus* Pers. (bright-flowered). Showy Sunflower. Similar to *H. rigidus* but generally taller, more leafy, and with phyllaries more lanceolate in shape and with tips generally acute. This "species" resembles hybrids between *H. rigidus* and *H. tuberosus* and probably originated through such hybridization. Michigan to Minnesota south to Indiana and Missouri; also occasional as an escape in the northeastern United States. Aug.–Sept. This is one of the most widely cultivated of the perennial sunflowers.

10. *H. tuberosus L.* (tuberous). Jerusalem Artichoke. Perennial from tubers, 5–14 feet tall; stems rough-hairy; leaves oblong-ovate to lance-ovate, cuneate to cordate at base, 5–12 inches long, hairy, serrate, opposite below, frequently alternate above; phyllaries lanceolate. Moist, alluvial soil, eastern North America. Sept. Not recommended as an ornamental since it is very aggressive and will take over the garden. Several different cultivars are known, based largely on tuber characteristics.

11. *H. decapetalus* L. (ten-petaled). Thin-Leaf Sunflower. Perennial from rhizomes, 2–5 feet tall, stems glabrous or slightly rough-hairy; leaves thin, ovate to ovate-lanceolate, 3–8 inches long, serrate, roughish above, slightly hairy beneath; phyllaries linear-lanceolate to lanceolate; rays pale yellow. Southeastern Canada to Iowa south to Georgia. July–Aug. This species normally grows in woodlands, and it is the only ornamental sunflower that tolerates considerable shade in the garden.

12. **H. × multiflorus* L. (many-flowered). Similar to the preceding, but stems slightly more hairy, leaves broader and thicker and often cordate at base; rays not as pale. *H. multiflorus* does not have a well-established common name and is not known in the wild. The plant is completely sterile as far as is known and probably arose as the result of a spontaneous cross of *H. annuus × H. decapetalus*. Several varieties are known, chiefly based on the extent and nature of the doubling of the flowers and the height.

13. *H. mollis* Lam. (soft hairy). Ashy Sunflower. Perennial from thick rhizomes, 2–5 feet tall; stem rather densely hairy; leaves mostly opposite, ovate, 3–6 inches long, usually cordate at base and clasping stem, soft-hairy; heads few; phyllaries lanceolate, pubescent; rays usually pale yellow. Massachusetts to Wisconsin south to Georgia and Texas. July–Aug. One of the more interesting-looking species.

14. **H. maximiliani* Schrad. (named for Maximilian, Prince of Wied, who traveled in North America in the early nineteenth century and made many botanical observations). Maximilian's Sunflower. Perennial from rhizomes; roots tuberous; stems several, 3–12 feet tall, rough; leaves mostly alternate, grayish-green, lanceolate, 3–10 inches long, more or less trough-shaped, rough, usually entire, sessile or nearly so; heads numerous on short stalks; phyllaries pubescent, linear-lanceolate; rays deep yellow. South-central Canada to Texas. The northern strains of this species are small in stature and flower quite early (June–July) when grown in Indiana, whereas the larger plants from the southern part of the range are quite late (Sept.–Oct.). By far the most ornamental races of the species are those from the Ozarks to Texas.

15. *H. giganteus* L. (gigantic). Giant Sunflower. Perennial from rhizomes; roots tuberous, 4–12 feet tall; stems several, rough-hairy; leaves mostly alternate, lanceolate, 3–8 inches long, shallowly toothed, nearly sessile, dark green; heads numerous on long stalks; phyllaries linear-lanceolate, ciliate; rays pale yellow.

Usually in moist soil, Ontario to Minnesota, south to Georgia and Kentucky. Aug.–Sept.

16. *H. grosseserratus* Martens (coarsely serrate). Sawtooth Sunflower. Perennial from rhizomes, roots tuberous, 5–14 feet tall, stems several, smooth, glaucous, leaves mostly alternate, lanceolate to 15 inches long, coarse-toothed to nearly entire, smooth above, finely woolly beneath, light to dark green, petioles 1–3 inches long; heads numerous on long stalks, phyllaries linear-lanceolate, usually glabrous, rays bright yellow. Massachusetts to Nebraska south to Kentucky and Texas. Aug.–Sept. Although this species is mentioned only infrequently in horticultural literature, it is actually one of the most striking. Hybrids of this species with *H. maximiliani* are more floriferous than either parent and hold great promise for those who enjoy tall sunflowers. (Neither the species epithet nor the little-used common name for this species is too apt; frequently the leaves are only slightly serrate or not serrate at all.)

17. **H. salicifolius* A. Dietr. (willow-leafed). Willow-Leaf Sunflower. Perennial from rhizomes, roots somewhat thickened, 6–12 feet tall, stems several, smooth, glaucous; leaves mostly alternate, linear-lanceolate to linear, 8–16 inches long, entire or obscurely serrate, sessile or short stalked; heads numerous; phyllaries linear-lanceolate to linear, glabrous; rays lemon yellow. Missouri and Kansas to north Texas. The extremely narrow leaves of this species are its outstanding feature. In the older literature it is known as *H. orgyalis* DC.

18. *H. angustifolius* L. (narrow-leafed). Swamp Sunflower. Perennial from slender rhizome, roots not thickened; stems hairy; 3–6 feet tall; leaves mostly alternate, basal leaves narrowly spatulate, those of the stem linear, 2–7 inches long, entire, margins usually inrolled, sessile, usually somewhat pubescent; phyllaries linear-lanceolate; rays bright yellow. Mostly wet places, Long Island to Missouri, south to Florida and Texas. Sept.–Oct.

CULTURAL REQUIREMENTS

One of the chief virtues of sunflowers is the ease with which they can be grown. Nearly all species, once successful germination has been accomplished, will do well in a variety of garden soils, although, as with most plants, the better the soil, the larger the plants. At times the germination of seeds offers some difficulties with most of the species except the giant sunflowers (*H. annuus* var. *macrocarpus*). Seeds may be sown where they are wanted in the garden in early spring and later thinned to the proper distance apart—usually two feet or more. Better germination of most of the species may be secured by planting the seeds in pots or flats early in the year and setting them outside where they may be subjected to temperature changes. A freezing and thawing action is apparently necessary to help break the achene coat in some species. All species, with the obvious exception of the sterile *H.* × *multiflorus* may be started from seeds, although seeds of some of the perennials, particularly *H. decapetalus*, are difficult to germinate even with freezing treatments.

After the second pair of true leaves appears or when the seedling is an inch or two high, it may be transplanted to its permanent spot in the garden. The usual care must be exercised in transplanting. The roots should be disturbed as little as possible, and the plants should be watered frequently until they are well established, usually in about two weeks. A slight frost will not damage most species, particularly if they have germinated outside, but some protection should be afforded the species from the southern United States when sharp temperature drops are expected.

Most of the perennial species may be propagated by dividing the rootstocks (rhizomes); this is, of course, the only way of growing *H.* × *multiflorus*. Plants of the perennials may be divided at the end of the first year. Indeed, it is recommended that they be divided every two or three years. The dead stalks of the plants may be removed after blooming is completed or the following spring before new growth commences.

After the sunflower is well established it needs only occasional weeding. Many sunflowers, in spite of their weedy nature, do not grow well with too much competition from other plants. Most of them are rank feeders, and applications of ordinary garden fertilizer are recommended, although if one wants small plants, it is to be avoided. The very tall species, *H. grosseserratus, H. salicifolius*, and *H. maximiliani*, may be cut back to near the ground in late spring or early summer if one prefers shorter, bushier plants, although actually the height of these plants is one of their outstanding features.

Seeds in most species are usually produced in abundance if more than one plant is grown. If more than one species is grown, hybridization may take place between them; thus if one saves seeds for planting, he may be in for some interesting results when he grows them.

The artificial production of a sunflower hybrid is relatively simple. Heads are bagged with sacks before the opening of the outermost row of flowers. A day or so later, after the flowers have opened, a head is broken off the plant that is to serve as the male parent, and the pollen is transferred to the plant that is to serve as the seed parent by lightly touching the heads together. The pollinated head is then rebagged to prevent bees from bringing in unwanted pollen. Sometimes bees try to land on the flowers while the bags are removed for pollinating, and if they are successful, the experiment must be started anew. Although the flowers of the sunflower are bisexual, emasculation is unnecessary in most sunflowers because the pollen of an individual plant will not function on its own flowers. The hybrid achenes are harvested a few weeks later, and, if the hybridization is successful, the achenes will be plump because of the presence of a seed inside; if not, the achene will be flat and empty. The hybridization of sunflowers and many other plants is so readily accomplished that such experiments may be carried out by the amateur with no other equipment than a few ordinary paper sacks (although they will have to be changed immediately after a rain before they break open).

Relatively little breeding work has been done to produce more ornamental sunflowers, compared to that done on zinnias, the marigolds, and the dahlias. With intentional breeding work, one may expect more beautiful sunflowers in the future. When this is accomplished, the sunflower may yet become a significant garden ornamental. After all, not too many years ago few would have predicted that the sunflower would become one of the world's most important sources of oil.

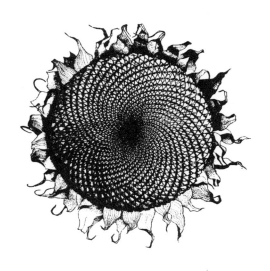

XV

What's in a Name

De sunflower ain't de daisy,
And de melon ain't de rose.
Why is dey all so crazy
To be sumpin' else dat grows?
—Edwin Milton Royle, "Doan't You Be What You Ain't"

So FAR it has been possible, although with some difficulty, to keep the use of scientific names to a minimum. Some have been used, however, and without apology, for there are many good reasons why we dignify plants with a Latin or Greek name. When one uses the word sunflower, he is generally referring to a plant of the genus *Helianthus*. We find, however, that some plants resembling a *Helianthus* have been called sunflowers. For example, the orange, or Mexican, sunflower is *Tithonia*; the false-sunflower is *Heliopsis*; and the tickseed sunflower is a *Bidens*. The last-named is sometimes called a bur marigold, but that name is little better, for the name marigold is more commonly used for the genus *Tagetes*. Many people, of course, call almost anything with yellow rays a sunflower—that is, if they do not try to call it some sort of daisy. (Incidentally, the name daisy has been used for ninety different genera of plants, but generally it refers to *Chrysanthemum leucanthemum* in America and to *Bellis perennis* in England.)

Therein lies the value of the genus name: it at once distinguishes a definite group of species that are generally more closely related to each other than to any other group of plants. In 1700 the French botanist Joseph Tournefort, was one of the first to employ the genus name consistently. The name sunflower may change as we move from country to country—*tournesol* in France, *girasol* in Spain and Italy, *Sonnenblume* in Germany, and подсолнечник in Russia but *Helianthus* means the same the world over. So it is with other plants—corn is used as the name for other cereals in England, and yet in this country it is used solely for Indian corn, or maize, which the botanist calls *Zea* to distinguish it from wheat (*Triticum*), oats (*Avena*), and other kinds of "corn."

When Shakespeare wrote, "That which we call a rose by any other name would smell as sweet," he was probably referring to the roses that belong to the genus *Rosa*, but the word rose has been used for many other plants. The California rose, the Christmas rose, the Confederate rose, the rose of heaven, and the moss rose or rose moss do not belong to the genus *Rosa*. The references to the rose in the King James version of the Bible in most cases are not to true roses (*Rosa*) at all.

The ragweed (*Ambrosia trifida*) of an earlier chapter is ragweed or giant ragweed to most people, but many farmers in southern Indiana call it horseweed. At the same time other people use the name horseweed to refer to another plant that botanists know as *Conyza canadensis*.

There is no need to labor the point at great length, for it should be clear by now that scientific names are a great deal more accurate than common names. Accurate identification may at times be a life-or-death matter. If someone has eaten nightshade berries, it could make a great deal of difference whether the berries came from *Solanum nigrum, S. dulcamara,* or *Atropa belladonna,* all of which are sometimes called nightshade but which vary considerably in the nature or the potency of their poison.

Just as the genus name *Helianthus* designates sunflowers, the addition of a species epithet lets us know what kind of sunflower we are dealing with. The use of species names for plants we owe largely to Linnaeus, for he consistently used a binomial consisting of the genus name and a specific epithet to refer to plants. For this reason the scientific naming of plants has been established as dating from 1753 with the publication of Linnaeus' work *Species Plantarum.* Before that time most of the herbalists had used long descriptive phrases for the plants, as was seen in the discussion of *H.* × *multiflorus* in an earlier chapter. All species of *Helianthus* may be called sunflowers, but many of them have no common name, and we must resort to the scientific name to distinguish them. The common sunflower is usually *H. annuus,* but a common sunflower in some parts of the country may be a quite different species. There are many different kinds of the common sunflower, as we have already seen, and it is desirable to designate some of these with still a third name, which is called a variety or subspecies. Thus we have the western wild sunflower, *H. annuus* subspecies *lenticularis*; the middle western and eastern weed, *H. annuus* subspecies *annuus* (which is probably the plant that Linnaeus had before him when he named the species originally); and the giant cultivated sunflower, *H. annuus* variety *macrocarpus.* Actually there is no more need to designate all the many different sorts of cultivated sunflowers with Latin names than there is to give blue- and brown-eyed people different scientific names.

The naming of cultivated plants in general follows the same rules as for wild plants. All plants—with the exception of hybrids—belong to a genus and species. In cultivated plants —both food and ornamental plants—each species may consist of a number of different types which we wish to distinguish. In the past these horticultural types were called varieties but this in no way distinguishes them from the varieties that occur in the wild, so in recent years the term cultivar (abbreviated, cv.) has been proposed for cultivated varieties. Moreover, to distinguish them from naturally occurring wild varieties which are designated with a Latin name the cultivar receives a "fancy" name. Thus we have *Rosa cathayensis*, Wedding Bells; *R. cathayensis*, Crimson Rambler; and so on. Thus the double-flowered sunflower, Sun Gold, is a cultivar of *H. annuus* subspecies *annuus*.[1]

Some people expect the scientific name to tell something about the plants—sometimes it does and sometimes it does not. *H. annuus* means annual sunflower, but as I pointed out earlier, the name does not help us in any way to distinguish it from the dozen other annual species. Plant names, like persons' names, do not need to tell us anything about the organisms but merely provide us a means of referring to them. Many plants are named after people—thus we have *H. maximiliani* and *H. nuttallii*. Ten sunflowers are named after persons, often after the man who first collected the plant.[2] (Incidentally, a botanist does not name a plant after himself. That honor is bestowed by others.) Some species are named for the region in which they grow; thus we find *H. californicus* and *H. floridanus*. Sometimes the name may actually be misleading or incorrect. In 1836 when it was named *H. occidentalis* ("western"), this sunflower may well have been considered a western species, but since it does not even get as far west as the Rockies, we would hardly consider it so today. *H. giganteus*, which was named by Linnaeus, is certainly a

---

[1] In horticultural papers the name of a cultivar is usually distinguished by placing it within single quotation marks, e.g., *H. annuus* 'Sun Gold.'

[2] This does not always lead to happy results. A. H. Curtiss, a botanical collector in Florida, collected a sunflower in 1900 which was sent to Merritt Fernald, of the Gray Herbarium at Harvard, for identification. Fernald concluded that the specimen represented a new species and intended to call it *H. curtissii*. However, before he was able to publish the diagnosis of the new species, another botanist described it under the name *H. agrestis*, and the sunflower had to bear that name, much to the disappointment of the original collector.

tall sunflower, but it is not at all gigantic when compared with certain forms of *H. annuus*. The species name *H. decapetalus* literally means "ten-petaled sunflower." Actually all sunflowers have five united petals in their flowers, and Linnaeus was referring to the fact that this sunflower has ten rays. Sometimes it does, but more often than not it may have more or less.

Then there are some species whose names are almost unpronounceable, such as *H. szyszylowiczii*. It has been shown, however, that the person who named this plant was mistaken, for it is not a true sunflower at all, but a member of the closely related genus *Viguiera*. When this plant is transferred to *Viguiera* it has to bear the name *V. lanceolata*—not because the other name is difficult to pronounce but because the name *V. lanceolata* was published several years earlier than *H. szyszylowiczii*.

The species names are precise and are accepted by botanists the world over. The names are seldom changed, and then only if there are compelling reasons to do so. The taxonomists have drawn up a code of rules to guide them in such matters. The example of *H. szyszylowiczii* is an illustration. Another is the showy sunflower that for a long time went under the name *H. orgyalis* (meaning having the height of a person with his arms extended). This plant was named by one of that eminent Swiss botanical family De Candolle, who was unaware that the same plant had been named *H. salicifolius* ("willow-leafed") by a German botanist, A. Dietrich, a few years earlier. When it was discovered that the two names referred to the same plant, the earlier name was selected, even though this species for years had gone under the name *H. orgyalis*. The "law of priority" holds in such cases.

It should be obvious that two species of the same genus cannot bear the same name. The sunflower with the snowy white leaves of Baja California was given the name *H. niveus* in 1889. This name was unknown to Georg Hieronymus, who in 1895 described a new species of sunflower from Peru under the name *H. niveus* because it also had a snowy-white pubescence on the leaves, although it differed in many other ways

Type specimen of *H. bolanderi*. The specimen was collected by Henry N. Bolander in Lake County, California, in 1864. Asa Gray, a professor at Harvard University, had it before him when he described the species in 1865. The specimen is preserved in the Gray Herbarium at Harvard.

from the Baja California plant and is clearly a different species. A few years later, when it was discovered that the two different sunflowers bore the same name, the late S. F. Blake, one of America's foremost authorities on the Compositae, renamed the South American plant *H. subniveus*. Today, with better communication of scientific work, it is unlikely that two species will be described under the same name.

In view of the great similarity between species, how can one be sure which plants Linnaeus and the other early botanists had before them a hundred years or more ago when most of the species were described? True, they left us descriptions, but they are often brief and sometimes not very helpful. More important is that they left us actual evidence in the form of dried specimens which were mounted on paper and preserved in herbaria. These flattened specimens may appear like so much dried hay to the layman (and to some nontaxonomic botanists, as well), but they provide a permanent record that a particular species name is attached to a particular plant. These "type" specimens and others like them are housed in universities and museums the world over. They are invaluable in helping determine the correct name for a plant and in many other ways as well. If one wants to study the sunflowers of South America, for example, it might be difficult to make an extended trip there. However, by borrowing these pressed plants from various institutions, the botanist can assemble for study specimens that would require years of personal travel and collection to accumulate. Moreover, these specimens can be dissected and studied in much the same way living plants are. If the flowers are boiled in water, they reassume their approximate natural shape and size. The color is sometimes lost, but if the specimen was collected by a careful botanist, the label will indicate the flower color, where and when it was collected, whether it was a tree, shrub, or herb, and other information. Although the specimen is dry and dead, in the hands of a skillful taxonomist it lives once again. The statement of Alfred C. Kinsey about his gall wasps, which he studied before he turned to human beings, applies equally well to the botanist's specimens: "Tho the taxonomists' specimens seem insignificant, the data tedious, and the dry-rot of the technic unendurable, the pinned specimens in the box are a bit of forests and the hills and the days where the drama of wasp life is unfolded, an evidence of ancient origins, mutating genes, and inexorable marches of evolution, an epitome of the enduring and everlasting changing entities which are species."

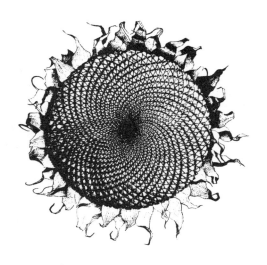

XVI

The Jerusalem Artichoke—
Neither from Jerusalem nor an Artichoke

IN THE earlier discussion of common names no mention was made of the Jerusalem artichoke. This was no oversight, for the Jerusalem artichoke deserves a chapter all its own. The name is certainly absurd, and its story will be taken up shortly. The Jerusalem artichoke (*H. tuberosus*), like the common sunflower, is a native, temperate North American plant that was used as food by certain Indians. It also is frequently a weed. The Jerusalem artichoke is one of our lesser cultivated plants and, like its relative, has spread around the world. But the rest of the story of the Jerusalem artichoke is quite different from that of the common sunflower. The seeds of the common sunflower are used for food, whereas the

The wild Jerusalem artichoke.

underground parts, the tubers,[1] of *H. tuberosus* have given it its gastronomical prominence. The common sunflower must be planted anew each year, but the tubers of the Jerusalem artichoke live over the winter in the ground and give rise to new plants in the spring. It also produces seeds, but the common means of propagation is through the planting of tubers.

Early man not only used seeds of wild plants for food but also utilized many other parts of plants, as we do today. The underground structures—bulbs, corms, tubers, and roots—frequently were important items of diet. Just as with the seed crops some of the tuber plants may have become weeds and eventually were graduated into the class of cultivated plants. Our records of their early history, however, are not as complete as those for the seed plants. Fleshy plant parts are rarely preserved archaeologically, and if roots or tubers were buried with the dead, they have long since disappeared in most places. We have excellent records of some tuberous crops from decorations on pottery, but the Jerusalem artichoke is not among them.

Some years ago Carl O. Sauer, in an interesting little book on agricultural origins, suggested that originally there were two sorts of primitive agriculture—one based on seed culture and the other on root culture. The discovery that edible root parts give rise to plants which in turn give rise to more is a fairly simple one, and he believed that agriculture based on root culture was probably practiced long before seed planting. The disturbance of the soil by digging for roots may actually benefit the growth of future plants and in a sense would be the first step in cultivation. The time and place of the origin of the practice of saving some of the roots or tubers for planting instead of eating them all are unknown. It was probably not until the plant was carried to a new area that there was any need for planting, because it would hardly be necessary to do so in the area in which the plant grew naturally.

[1] Tubers, although produced underground, are actually stems. Another, better-known, example of the tuber is the Irish potato.

Tubers of the Jerusalem artichoke: from wild plant (*above*), from domesticated plant (*below*).

Today the Jerusalem artichoke is cultivated in many places around the world and grows naturally throughout most of northeastern North America. Within the latter area we find several records of Indians using the tubers (or "roots" as they were usually called), for food, but it is not always clear whether the tubers came from wild or cultivated plants.

The first written notice of the plant by a European appeared in 1605, when Samuel de Champlain mentioned roots with the taste of artichokes which the Indians cultivated. It is generally agreed that this is a reference to *H. tuberosus* and that the observation was made at what is now Nausett Harbor, Massachusetts. Can we be certain that the Indians were actually "cultivating" the plants in the sense that we use the word today, or were they simply taking advantage of weeds

174

that had an affinity for the fields of man? Unfortunately, Champlain gave us no more details. The Indians, of course, could have cultivated the plant, and it might still have not necessarily been domesticated, for a distinction can be made between "cultivated" and "domesticated," although the words are often used interchangeably. A wild plant can be transplanted to a garden, but that does not make it a domesticated plant, which can result only after some time of cultivation and selection. The common sunflower was clearly domesticated by the Indians, but the evidence for the Jerusalem artichoke is not as certain.

The wild Jerusalem artichoke has small tubers, whereas those from the forms cultivated today have much larger tubers. So some information about the size of the tubers of the first plants grown in Europe might be helpful in determining whether the Indians had indeed domesticated the plant. The first such description is apparently by one Marc Lescarbot, a French lawyer who visited America in 1607 and returned to France with Champlain. He wrote that he found there "a certain kind of root as big as one's fist, very good to eat," as one translation gives it. The word fist is given as *pain* in the original French. *Pain*, of course, means "bread" and perhaps the translator considered *pain* a misprint for *poing*, French for "fist." If, indeed, the first artichokes to reach Europe were as big as a man's fist, there could be little doubt that they were from a domesticated type. If, on the other hand, bread is actually intended, its meaning is uncertain. In 1617, Lescarbot again wrote of the plant, saying that the roots were the size of turnips or truffles. This is hardly precise, for turnips and truffles can vary considerably in size, but I would guess that they were larger than wild artichokes. In other early accounts of the plant in Europe the tubers are compared to hen's eggs and chestnuts, the latter being from a dried tuber. These descriptions are not necessarily from the same plant source as Lescarbot's, for there were probably other introductions of the plant into Europe from America after voyages to America began to be made with some regularity.

The base of the plant of *H. giganteus*, showing the enlarged roots.

While at this late date it may be impossible to learn much more about the type of Jerusalem artichokes the Indians were using several centuries ago, I think it is likely that the plant was cultivated at times and that a form with tubers slightly larger than those of wild types had evolved through selection by the Indians. It is likely, however, that more intensive selection was practiced in Europe after several different introductions had been made from America and that much of the plant's improvement is fairly recent. But even today the Jerusalem artichoke is far less "domesticated" than the giant sunflower, which has completely lost its ability to perpetuate itself without man's aid. While we may not be able to determine the exact extent to which the Indians cultivated the Jerusalem artichoke, it seems most likely that they may have been responsible for its introduction into new areas and that its distribution as a wild plant was considerably enlarged as a result.

Certain other species of perennial sunflowers produce enlarged roots—true roots and not tubers—that were also gathered for food by some Indians. These have sometimes been confused with the Jerusalem artichoke. Lewis and Clark in their expedition related that "when we stopped for dinner the squaws went out and after penetrating with a sharp stick the holes of the gopher, brought to us a quantity of wild artichokes which the mice collect and hoard in great numbers." This plant has been identified as *H. giganteus*, which is reported as a food plant in other areas of the United States, but since this species does not occur in the West, in all probability Lewis and Clark ate the roots of *H. nuttallii*, a species closely related to *H. giganteus*.

H. tuberosus is a polyploid species, having 102 chromosomes. It is sometimes possible to determine exactly the ancestry of the polyploids if the progenitors are not extinct. Most polyploids have two different species as parents which, through hybridization, gave rise to a hybrid in which chromosome doubling occurred. The botanists can sometimes repeat nature's experiments. The two plants suspected of being the parents of the polyploid can be artificially crossed, and the resulting hybrid can be enticed to double its chromosomes by treatment with a drug known as colchicine. The resulting plant should be similar to the naturally occurring polyploid if the botanist has been correct in his hypothesis about the parents. Such critical experiments have not yet been carried out with the Jerusalem artichoke, but some preliminary work has been done, and a hypothesis can be erected that eventually will be subjected to experimental verification.

In all probability the Jerusalem artichoke acquired its 102 chromosomes as a result of hybridization between a species with 34 and another with 68 chromosomes. Such hybridization would produce a triploid plant that, following chromosome doubling, would become a hexaploid. The problem is to decide which of the many species of sunflowers are its ancestors. Some species, such as the South American ones and those of the western United States, appear unlikely candidates because of their geographical position. Of the remaining species of the eastern United States many can virtually be eliminated because they possess characters quite unlike those found in the Jerusalem artichoke. The 68-chromosome species almost certainly has to be one of three closely related species, *H. decapetalus*, *H. hirsutus*, or *H. strumosus*, all common in the central and eastern United States. Of these, *H. hirsutus* most nearly resembles *H. tuberosus* and seems to be the most likely candidate for one parent.

The determination of the second parent, the species with 34 chromosomes, is a more difficult problem. Some years ago it was suggested that the common sunflower, *H. annuus*, or a species similar to it, was one of the parents. If this is correct, then it almost certainly means that the Indians were responsible for bringing this species into contact with the 68-chromosome species, for in all probability the two species did not have overlapping distributions until the common sunflower was introduced into the middle and eastern regions of the United States. If the common sunflower is one of the parents, then it is likely that *H. tuberosus* is a very youthful species, only a few thousand years old, and has acquired an extensive range in a relatively short time. Although a polyploid plant most likely would appear more similar to the parent that furnished the greater number of chromosomes, some evidence of the second parent might be expected. There is no clear indication that *H. annuus* is involved, as far as the appearance is concerned.

The other possibility for the second parent, assuming that it is not an extinct species, would be a diploid perennial sunflower of the central and eastern United States, of which there are a great number of species. Of these it seems that ones such as *H. giganteus* or *H. grosseserratus*, when combined with *H. hirsutus*, would result in a sunflower similar in appearance and ecology to the Jerusalem artichoke.

Although the origin of the Jerusalem artichoke remains obscure, its recent history is better understood. Although Champlain appears to have been the first European to mention the Jerusalem artichoke, the credit for its introduction into Europe probably belongs either to Marc Lescarbot, previously mentioned, or to Louis Hébert, an apothecary who afterwards was the first permanent resident of Quebec. The plant was soon adopted as a food plant in France, and from there it spread to other parts of Europe. It was introduced into Sweden in 1638 by M. J. Franck, who believed that eating it would increase the production of human sperm. Apparently it was not adopted as a cultivated plant by the early pioneers in its own country, but it is recorded that because of its aggressive tendencies it proved itself a nuisance in pioneer gardens.

In England shortly after its introduction the tubers of this prolific plant immediately became popular and were prepared in a variety of ways, as indicated by various English herbalists. Tobias Venner in 1622 mentioned that "artichokes of Jerusalem is a roote usually eaten with butter, vinegar, and pepper, by itself, or together with other meates." John Parkinson in 1629 wrote that "being put into seething water they are soon boyled tender, which after they be peeled, sliced and stewed with butter, and a little wine was a dish for a Queene." John Goodyer a few years later added new ways of serving them: "These roots are dressed divers ways, some boile them in water, and after stew them with sacke and butter, adding a little ginger. Others bake them in pies, putting marrow, Dates, Ginger, Raisons of the sun, Sacke, etc."

It is interesting to note that another American tuber crop, the Irish potato, introduced into Europe even earlier than the Jerusalem artichoke, did not immediately meet with much favor and had to wait some time before it gained acceptance as a food plant. Today, of course, it is one of the major crops of Europe. In spite of the Jerusalem artichoke's auspicious early reception, it was never to become an important food plant. Some of the reasons for this may perhaps be found in the comments of the same herbalists who were quoted earlier:

"It breedeth melancholy and is somewhat nauseous and fulsome to the stomacke, and thereful very hurtful to the melancholick, and them that have weak stomackes" (Venner). "The Jerusalem artichokes by reason of their increasing [have] grown so common here that even the most vulgar begin to despise them, whereas when they were first received among us were dainties for a Queene" (Parkinson). ". . . but in my judgement which way soever they be drest and eaten, they stir and cause a filthy loathsome stinking wind within the body, thereby causing the belly to be pained and tormented; and are a meat more fit for swine, than man" (Goodyer). A century later Philip Miller was also to comment on the "windy" property of the Jerusalem artichoke.

However, in spite of the objections of the early writers, the plant continued to be used as a food and remained popular in certain areas of Europe. A few people in the United States have long cultivated it, and currently the plant seems to be enjoying a new popularity. Bottled artichoke "pickles" can be purchased in some stores. Wild-food fanciers enjoy eating the tubers of the plant.

The tubers have been recommended as good food for diabetics. Unlike most of our root crops, the Jerusalem artichoke contains inulin instead of starch. During digestion the inulin is converted into fructose, a sugar that can be handled by diabetics. However, it is not listed among the foods recommended for diabetics in most modern works on the subject. The Jerusalem artichoke has been used for the commercial preparation of fructose and also as a source of industrial alcohol. However, its greatest use at present seems to be the one suggested by Goodyer—food for swine.

Since it has limited economic importance, the plant has not been given much attention by plant breeders, and one does not find the diversity of types that are found in most domesticated plants. It is by no means a uniform species, however, and again we find the greatest variation in the character for which it is grown. Just as the common sunflower shows considerable variation in the achene, the Jerusalem artichoke shows great diversity in the tubers. White-, yellow-, and purple-skinned tubers in addition to red-skinned ones, which seem to be the commonest type in the wild, are known. The shape and size of the tuber also vary considerably.

In a previous chapter it was pointed out that through the use of hybrids with the Jerusalem artichoke the Russians had secured disease resistance in the cultivated sunflower. Indeed, this may be one of the plant's greatest contributions to man's welfare. But something may yet happen to make the Jerusalem artichoke a truly significant plant to man. As mentioned above, the plant has been used as a source of sugar. A quarter of a century ago a Swedish plant breeder investigated the possibility of using the hybrid between the Jerusalem artichoke and the common sunflower, sometimes called the Sunchoke, as a sugar crop. The hybrid is more vigorous than either parent and, like the Jerusalem artichoke, is a perennial. The idea was that the stems would be harvested and the tubers would be left in the ground. Thus there would be no need to replant the crop every year as must be done with man's Temperate Zone sugar crop, the sugar beet. It was thought the Sunchoke might come to rival the sugar beet, but little has been heard of it since the original idea was advanced.

Like many hybrids, the Sunchoke is almost totally sterile. Seeds are rarely produced—but what it lacks in seeds it more than makes up for in tubers, which are abundantly produced, a single plant yielding several pounds. The tubers are edible and seem to lack some of the objectionable properties of the ordinary Jerusalem artichokes. The Russians claim to have produced such a hybrid with tubers equal to those of the Jerusalem artichoke and seeds as good as those of the common cultivated sunflower. Thus both ends of the plant could be eaten. It is not clear from the accounts that I have seen of this remarkable plant whether it was secured through ordinary sexual hybridization—that is, the union of the sperm of one species with the egg of the other—or through "vegetative hybridization,"—grafting. It would be possible to graft a stem of the common sunflower onto the root stock of the Jerusalem artichoke and secure a plant that would produce tubers and seeds, just as a tomato-potato graft "hybrid" will produce both potatoes and tomatoes. The plant could not reproduce itself, however, since the tubers would give rise to Jerusalem artichokes and the seeds would give rise to common sunflowers. Moreover, the "hybrid" would not give yields of either tubers or seeds that would be expected in either parent, respectively. The Russian claim was made in the days when Lysenko was in charge of Soviet Union agriculture, and I have seen nothing about the plant recently.

For the present the Jerusalem artichoke's greatest claim to

fame will have to rest on its common name. The plant which botanists call *H. tuberosus*, in common with other cultivated plants, has had a number of vernacular names, but two stand out above the others—Jerusalem artichoke, which is used in most English-speaking countries, and *topinambour*, which is used in France and in a few other European countries. Both names are equally ridiculous. For that reason in 1918 the *Gardener's Chronicle*, an English publication, offered a prize for a new common name for the plant. Today the plant is still called Jerusalem artichoke and *topinambour*, but the contest indirectly resulted in two excellent studies of the history of the names by C. C. Lacaita and Redcliffe Salaman, both of which have been consulted for this account.

Since the name *topinambour* is more easily explained, let us start with it. The plant, as we have seen in the last chapter, was introduced from America to France in the early years of the seventeenth century. A few years after its introduction, six natives of a Brazilian island were taken to France, probably for political reasons relating to colonization in the New World. The Topinambous, as the natives were called, became the rage of Paris. They were presented to the queen, and those who survived the first two months were baptized with King Louis, then aged twelve, as sponsor, and French wives were selected for them. Exactly how the name of these natives became attached to the new plant is not known, but it has been supposed that some energetic street hawker appropriated the name for the plant to capitalize on the advertising value of the Topinambous. Similar practices, of course, are not unknown in the commercial world today.

Not everyone was happy with the new name, as is attested to by the account of Lescarbot:

When it was essential to find the wherewithal to live [in the New World], God caused us to find roots,[2] which to-day one can find served as a luxury on many a table in France, which some people

---

[2] Salaman, an Englishman, who translated this passage, comments that the Frenchman was "dilating on Providence's obvious bias towards the French" in making this statement.

in Paris, ignorantly call Topinamboux whilst others, more correctly, "Canada," for it is from there that they came here. . . . a plague on those who caused the hawkers in Paris to call them Topinamboux.

Since Lescarbot may have been responsible for the introduction of the plant into France, he perhaps would be justified in registering a complaint.

This name even caused confusion among the botanists who ought to have known better, and for a time South America was regarded as the original home of the plant. No less an authority than Linnaeus gives Brazil as the homeland of the plant in his *Species Plantarum* of 1753, although in an earlier work he had assigned it to Canada.

The name Jerusalem artichoke requires a somewhat lengthier explanation. In 1622, Venner in the first mention of the sunflower in English used the name "Artichokes of Jerusalem." In 1629, Parkinson called the tubers "Potato's of Canada" and made the comment that "we in England, from some ignorant and idle head have called them 'Artichokes of Jerusalem.' " In spite of this early complaint about the name it persisted, and we even find, logically enough perhaps, that soup made from the tubers was called Palestine soup. In 1807, Sir J. E. Smith put forth the idea that the name Jerusalem artichoke was a corruption of the Spanish name *Girasole articiocco* (actually the Italian name). This explanation gained wide acceptance and was not challenged until recently.

The artichoke part of the name causes little difficulty, for both Champlain and Lescarbot mentioned that in taste the tuber resembled the globe artichoke. The latter is also a member of the sunflower family but belongs to the thistle tribe and hence is not closely related to the sunflower. In addition, the bracts surrounding the flower head, rather than the underground parts of the true artichoke, are eaten. However, on the basis of taste alone we may accept the transfer of the name artichoke to the sunflower as plausible.

The difficulty then lies with "Jerusalem." We might be able to go along with Smith and believe that somehow the English twisted the word *girasol* (meaning "turn as the sun") into Jerusalem were it not for the fact that the sunflower probably reached England before it did Italy and certainly before the plant had acquired the name *girasol*. Salaman has marshaled convincing evidence for this. The earliest use of *girasol* was for the fire opal, and the name *girasol* was used for the castor bean long before it was attached to the sunflower.

One suggestion put forward—the most logical to date—is based on information gleaned from an herbal published in 1618 in which we learn that one Petrus Hondius planted a small, shriveled-up tuber in his garden at Ter Neusen, Holland, and that it multiplied in an amazing fashion. The tubers were distributed, and among other names we find that they were called "artichoke-apples of Ter-Neusen." This name may well have followed the plant to England, where Ter-Neusen somehow became converted to Jerusalem, a name that would have more meaning to the English.

As for the outcome of the *Gardener's Chronicle* contest, ten persons submitted the name sunroot, which in the estimation of the judges was the best. Probably none of the judges nor the contestants were aware that certain Indians of Virginia already had a name for the plant, *kaischuc penauk*, which means "sunroot." The name sunroot perhaps is more appropriate than either Jerusalem artichoke or *topinambour*, even though the part of the plant eaten is definitely not a root. In any event, this name was never adopted and the plant is still called Jerusalem artichoke and *topinambour*. Salaman has provided a fitting close: "The familiar names topinambour and Jerusalem Artichoke will assuredly be with us to the end, perpetual witness of the incurable illogicality which does so much to lighten the common drab of man's life here below."

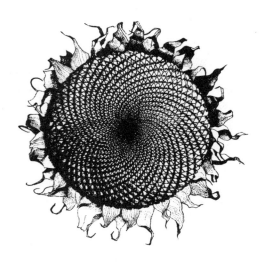

Bibliographical Notes

While no attempt has been made to include a complete list of works consulted, some of the principal references, some suggestions for additional reading, and some "footnote materials" are given below:

Foreword
The story of how I became involved with sunflowers is given in greater detail in Charles B. Heiser, Jr., "Student Days with Edgar Anderson, or How I Came to Study Sunflowers," *Annals of the Missouri Botanical Garden*, Vol. LIX (1972), 362–72.

Chapter I
The material on the "Kansas-Iowa sunflower controversy" came chiefly from the press: *Des Moines Register*, March 9, 15, 17, 27, 1969; *Kansas City Times* and *Kansas City Star*, March 26, 1969.
Woodson's story about Standley appeared in Louis Williams

(ed.), *Homage to Standley* (Chicago, Chicago Natural History Museum, 1963).

Chapter II

I have not done justice to the sunflower in art. An indication of its importance in the Victorian period will be found in Elizabeth Aslin, *The Aesthetic Movement: Prelude to Art Nouveau* (New York, Praeger, 1969). She thinks that it is possible that Oscar Wilde was to some extent responsible for the choice of the sunflower as an aesthetic symbol. Wilde in a lecture in New York in 1882 on the English Renaissance of art said: "You have heard . . . of two flowers connected with the aesthetic movement in England and said (I assure you, erroneously) to be the food of some aesthetic young men. Well, let me tell you the reason we love the lily and the sunflower. . . . It is because these two lovely flowers are in England the two most perfect models of design, the most naturally adapted for decorative art—the gaudy leonine beauty of the one and the precious loveliness of the other giving to the artist the most entire and perfect joy."

Chapter IV

A more detailed treatment of the sunflowers of the Indians with a long list of references may be found in Charles B. Heiser, Jr., "The Sunflower Among the North American Indians," *Proceedings* of the American Philosophical Society, Vol. VC (1951), 432–48.

The account of the Hidatsa sunflower is from Gilbert L. Wilson, "Agriculture of the Hidatsa Indians, an Indian Interpretation," University of Minnesota *Studies in Social Services*, No. 9 (1917).

Chapter V

The account of the adoption of the sunflowers by the Russians is from Melvin R. Gilmore, "Plant Vagrants in America," *Papers* of the Michigan Academy of Sciences, Arts and Letters, Vol. XV (1931), 65–79.

More information about the early history of the sunflower in Europe is provided by P.M. Žukovskij in his *Cultivated Plants and Their Wild Relatives* (1950): "The earliest record of them is the seeds brought by the Spanish expedition to New Mexico in 1510 and sown in the Madrid botanic garden. It was described by Lobel in 1576 and for many years its origin was wrongly ascribed to Peru. It was first distributed as an ornamental plant; it was introduced into Russia in the 18th century by Peter the Great and was used for chewing as well as for ornamental purposes; selection for large heads led to fasciation and in this way the unbranched forms with large heads were developed. The first suggestion of producing oil from the seeds came in the Proceedings of the Russian Academy in 1779 and the method was developed by Bolotov, Bokurev and others. Selection for oil content was started in 1860." This quotation is taken from the abridged translation by P. S. Hudson and published by the Commonwealth Agricultural Bureaux, Farnham Royal, England, in 1962. I have not seen the original work in Russian, but some comment is called for nevertheless. It hardly seems that there could have been a Spanish expedition to New Mexico in 1510; Old Mexico was not conquered until a few years after that date. Also, as I think I have shown in the text, unbranched forms of the sunflower with large heads went directly to Europe from America, and I assume that they then went to Russia. I remain skeptical of the statement that "selection for large heads led to fasciation."

Chapter VI

Much of the information on the recent development of sunflowers has been drawn from various papers in the *Proceedings* of the Fourth International Conference on Sunflowers, 1970 (Dalton Gandy, Chairman, National Cottonseed Products Association, Memphis, Tenn.). For earlier accounts see Eric D. Putt, "Sunflowers," *Field Crop Abstracts*, Vol. XVI (1963), 1–6, and E. F. Hurt, *Sunflowers for Food, Fodder and Fertility* (London, Faber and Faber, 1948).

Chapter VIII

Additional details may be found in Charles B. Heiser, Jr., "The Origin and Development of the Cultivated Sunflower," *American Biology Teacher*, Vol. XVII (1955), 161–67. Richard A. Yarnell, in a paper to be published in *The Handbook of North American Indians* by the Smithsonian Institution, has brought together all of the reference material relating to archaeological sunflowers and also discusses at length the other wild and semicultivated plants of the North American Indians.

Chapter IX

For the papers on seed longevity, see H. T. Darlington and G. P.

Steinbauer, "The Eighty Year Period for Dr. Beal's Seed Viability Experiment," *American Journal of Botany*, Vol. XLVIII (1961), 321–25; Ødum, Søren, "Germination of Ancient Seeds," *Dansk Botanisk Arkiv*, Vol. XXIV (1965), 1–70; A. E. Porsild, C. R. Harington, and G. A. Mulligan, "*Lupinus arcticus* Wats, grown from seeds of Pleistocene age," *Science*, Vol. CLVIII (1967), 113–14. While there can be no question about the results of Beal's experiments, some doubts might be raised in regard to the other reports.

The paper by Wilson and Rice, "Allelopathy as Expressed by *Helianthus annuus* and Its Role in Old Field Succession," appeared in the *Bulletin* of the Torrey Botanical Club, Vol. XCV (1968), 432–48.

Chapter X

For the reader interested in a good modern account of evolutionary theory, I recommend G. Ledyard Stebbins, *Processes of Organic Evolution*, 2d ed. (Englewood Cliffs, N.J., Prentice-Hall, 1971).

Chapter XI

A large number of papers dealing with hybridization of sunflowers have appeared. A selection is given here: Charles B. Heiser, Jr., "Hybridization in the Annual Sunflowers: *Helianthus annuus* × *H. debilis* var. *cucumerifolius*," *Evolution*, Vol. V (1951), 42–51. R. C. Jackson and A. T. Guard, "Natural and Artificial Hybridization between *Helianthus mollis* and *H. occidentalis*," *American Midland Naturalist*, Vol. LVIII (1957), 422–33. R. W. Long, "Biosystematics of Two Perennial Species of *Helianthus* (Compositae). II. Natural Populations and Taxonomy," *Brittonia*, Vol. XIII (1960), 129–41. D. M. Smith and A. T. Guard, "Hybridization Between *Helianthus divaricatus* and *H. microcephalus*," *Brittonia*, Vol. X (1958), 137–45.

Chapter XII

For an account of the early work on hybridization in relation to plant improvement see H. F. Roberts, *Plant Hybridization Before Mendel* (Princeton, Princeton University Press, 1929).

There are now available several accounts of Lysenko's work. An excellent one is Z. A. Medvedev, *The Rise and Fall of T. D. Lysenko* (trans. by I. Michael Lerner, New York, Columbia University Press, 1969).

For an English account of some of the Russian work in plant breeding of sunflowers see G. V. Pustovoit, "Interspecific Hybridization as a Method of Sunflower Selection," *Soviet Genetics*, Vol. II (1966), 33–39.

Leclercq's work on the cytoplasmic male sterile sunflowers appeared in *Annales de L'Amélioration des Plantes*, Vol. XIX (1969), 99–106.

Chapter XIII

Cockerell's own accounts of the development of the red sunflower may be found in *Popular Science Monthly* (April, 1920) and in *American Museum Journal*, Vol. XVIII (1918), 38–47.

More about *H. multiflorus* is presented in Charles B. Heiser, Jr., and D. M. Smith, "The Origin of *Helianthus multiflorus*," *American Journal of Botany*, Vol. XLVII (1960), 860–65.

Chapter XIV

Keys for identification, descriptions, and illustrations of all the North American species of sunflowers are found in Charles B. Heiser, Jr., D. M. Smith, Sarah Clevenger, and W. C. Martin, "The North American Sunflowers (*Helianthus*)," *Memoirs* of the Torrey Botanical Club, Vol. XXII (1969), 1–218.

Chapter XV

Those interested in learning more about the scientific naming of plants should consult P. H. Davis and V. H. Heywood, *Principles of Angiosperm Taxonomy* (Princeton, N.J., Van Nostrand, 1963).

Chapter XVI

Accounts of the history of the Jerusalem artichoke are given by C. C. Lacaita, "The 'Jerusalem Artichoke,'" *Bulletin of Miscellaneous Information*, Kew Royal Botanic Gardens (1919), 321–39, and by R. N. Salaman, "Why 'Jerusalem' Artichoke?" *Journal of the Royal Horticultural Society*, n.s., Vol. LXV (1940), 338–48, 376–83.

For polyploidy in relation to the origin of perennial sunflowers see Heiser and D. M. Smith, "Species Crosses in *Helianthus*. II. Polyploid Species," *Rhodora*, Vol. LXVI (1964), 344–58.

The book by Sauer is *Agricultural Origins and Dispersals* (New York, American Geographical Society, 1952).

A popular article by Euell Gibbons (*Natural History Magazine*,

February, 1971, 14–21) deserves some comment since it contains a number of inaccurate statements regarding sunflowers (see "Letters," *Natural History Magazine*, May, 1971, 92–93). His article, entitled "On the Trail of the Three Sisters," attracted my attention, for the drawing labeled "Sunflower *H. annuus*" was clearly not of that species (which I later learned was the magazine's and not Gibbons' fault). As I read on, I learned that the "three sisters" were corn, squash, and beans and that "only beans were indigenous to the area [the United States]." The last statement was in error, for the common beans, *Phaseolus vulgaris*, came to the United States from Mexico, according to the evidence of ethnobotanists. Some of Gibbons' ideas concerning the geography of the Jerusalem artichoke also could not be accepted. He maintained that the Jerusalem artichoke was cultivated by the Indians in Arizona, the evidence being that it is found near Indian ruins in that state. Even if it were present near Indian ruins, it would not necessarily mean that the Indians had either introduced it or cultivated it, but there is no scientific record that the Jerusalem artichoke was known in Arizona. I have never seen the plant there in my own field work, nor is it recorded in the complete *Arizona Flora*, by T. H. Kerney and R. H. Peebles (Berkeley, University of California Press, 1960). Gibbons did not give the source of his "evidence." One can hardly doubt that he might have seen a sunflower growing near Indian ruins in Arizona, but, in view of the difficulty of accurately identifying sunflowers, one can question his determination of the species. Possibly it was *H. nuttallii*, which has been confused with the Jerusalem artichoke and is known to occur as a wild plant in Arizona.

Gibbons was of the opinion that the Jerusalem artichoke is "in the process of giving up the ability to bear viable seeds" because he has observed several patches and never has seen any evidence of a seedling. Again, I do not doubt his observation, but I do not think it leads to the conclusion he has reached. The best way to determine whether a plant is producing seeds is to look for seeds, not seedlings. Many perennial plants may produce good seeds, and, for one reason or another, seedlings may not become established in some years. I have examined many populations of Jerusalem artichokes and have found that in many places the plants bear heads full of seed; moreover, the seeds are viable, as has been borne out by germination experiments. I have also on occasion seen seedlings in nature. I should add that at times I have found populations of Jerusalem artichokes in which not a single seed could be found. There is a very simple explanation for this. It takes cross-pollination between two genetically different individuals for seed production to occur in this species. Since a whole patch or population of Jerusalem artichokes may be derived from the introduction of a single original tuber, all the plants produced from it would be the same genetically, and hence no seeds could be produced. The cultivated Jerusalem artichoke also may fail to produce seeds at times when it is grown outside its normal climatic range.

In another section Gibbons maintained that "the domestic type [of *H. annuus*] planted in the wild quickly reverts to the wild type. I have seen this happen several times." This I find most interesting but difficult to believe because it is contrary to my own observations. When a sunflower is cultivated in a garden, even if the seeds are not harvested, it seldom comes up by itself the next year. Occasionally volunteer plants may appear, and they are usually similar to their parents except that they may be smaller in size. The smaller size is not a genetic change but a vegetative modification that most likely results from competition with other plants that are ordinarily eliminated in the cultivated garden. On occasion I have seen sunflowers persist in an abandoned garden for more than one year, and, while they may be branched, they are like the cultivated sunflower in other characters. It is probable that the branched condition is not the same as that in wild sunflowers, for several genes are known to control the expression of this character. If, indeed, it is found that sunflowers appear to have reverted to the wild type (which I have never observed), that again could have a simple explanation. When domesticated sunflowers are grown near wild sunflowers, cross-pollination may take place between the two varieties, and the resulting hybrids could occupy the area originally inhabited by the cultivated sunflower. Such hybrids in turn could backcross to the wild type, so that in time plants essentially like the wild ones would appear in the area where the sunflower was once cultivated. Such sunflowers then would not be reversions, as Gibbons might assume, but hybrid derivatives. The domesticated sunflower, like many, if not most, domesticated species of plants, is ill-adapted to survive in the wild.

While Gibbons may be deficient in his knowledge of the botany of sunflowers, he does present several interesting ways of using wild plants. My wife has tried several of his recipes, and we have found the resulting dishes good.

191

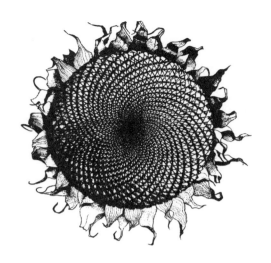

Index

193